SPROUTS,
SHOOTS &
MICROGREENS

SPROUTS, SHOOTS & MICROGREENS

Tiny Plants to Grow and Eat in Your Home Kitchen

LINA WALLENTINSON

PHOTOGRAPHY BY LENNART WEIBULL
TRANSLATED BY GUN PENHOAT

Skyhorse Publishing

CONTENTS

GROWING FOR THE IMPATIENT

At the grocery store, we're typically drawn to the colorful displays of fresh fruits and vegetables. Spicy radishes, shiny apples, and sunny lemons all brazenly clamor for our attention.

Meanwhile, we easily miss the shelves where the dried lentils, beans, and peas can be found. Now and again we'll grab a packet of red lentils for a quick soup, but what are those dried khaki mung beans and yellow peas good for?

At first, that was my thought when, in my capacity as food writer, I was asked to come up with an article about beans and peas. This meant I would have to hang around those shelves a little longer. Somewhat half-heartedly, I picked up, prodded, and looked over the labels of the packets, their contents ranging in color from dull brown and yellow to mild green and muted orange.

Gradually, as I learned more about legumes, it dawned on me that there was actually more life here than in the vegetable aisle, even though this life was dormant; hundreds of small seeds within these packets were just waiting to start sprouting. I began to grow sprouts and shoots as often as I could. Some shot up but tasted only okay, while others didn't want to go along with my plan at all. However, most of them turned into tasty sprouts and crisp shoots with surprising ease.

That bag of mung beans took on a whole new level of significance. These are the kings of all sprouts: they always produce a reliable harvest, and in four days or so become hearty bunches of crisp sprouts ready to be tossed into the nearest pad thai or other stir-fry. And dried peas—like ugly ducklings, these bashful soup peas grow into the city's most elegant shoots within a short couple of weeks. And let's not forget about lentils, which will grow into a tasty tangle after only two or three days.

Once you notice there is indeed life on the store shelf stocked with dried legumes, you'll discover more varieties. Take buckwheat, for example; while dry as dust, it only needs a bit of love and plenty of water to quickly soften into nice, triangular-shaped seeds with a timid little mini-sprout, at which point it's ready to perk up any salad or enhance a smoothie. Sunflower seeds, too, react without much prompting: you can almost see the sprouts begin to grow the moment they connect to water.

I've never really tended a garden, even though I have one. Everything happens so slowly. I've just never been interested in waiting several weeks—sometimes months—without any guarantee that things will come up.

However, sprouts and shoots are quick and prolific, and become instant food! They're an impatient grower's dream!

INTRODUCTION
HOMEGROWN IN A FLASH

Sprouts, shoots, and microgreens. They all start out as a small, dry grain. And when placed in water, they all begin to grow. Within a few days, crisp tails emerge and the sprouts are ready to be munched on.

If the sprouts are left to keep growing, they'll turn into green shoots. Unlike sprouts, which are eaten whole, the shoots are snipped off—you only consume the stalk and the leaves. The seed and the root have already done their bit, so to speak. *Microgreens* is a word that is becoming more and more familiar to us, and it simply designates the shoots from a seed.

Any seed can be sprouted, since that is a seed's inherent purpose. For this book, I've chosen seeds I believe produce the best-tasting sprouts and shoots and are easy to work with. I've also tried to ensure they're easy to get, preferably those used for food and available at any well-stocked grocery store. As for shoots, I couldn't resist including a few that can only be, for the most part, purchased online. They're definitely worth it, though—they taste so good! (They have a great peppery flavor that's almost addictive.)

Some seeds are developed specifically for growing into sprouts and shoots. You'll usually find information on their germination rate on the package, and the average rate of seed germination is given as a percentage. Germination should exceed 90 percent. As for seeds bought at grocery stores, such as lentils, peas, and buckwheat, the rate of germination will vary, but in my experience, it's usually satisfactory. Be sure to check that the seeds you buy are viable, i.e., that they're not past their sell-by dates. Choose young seeds over older ones, because while dry seeds typically keep longer overall, germination rates do diminish with time. If the seeds are stored in a place that's too warm, their germination rate will also be negatively affected. Since it's difficult to know at what temperature seeds have been stored, it's always prudent to select younger seeds.

There's no difference in germination rates between organic seeds and those that are grown conventionally. Opting for one over the other is a matter of personal preference.

Sprouts and shoots are smart and healthy foods. Eating them is better for you than just eating the seeds. A lot happens during the growth. The dry seed shields itself in a lot of ways from getting eaten before it has a chance to sprout. It holds on to its vital minerals and proteins with all its strength. Once it starts growing, however, frantic activity ensues. The future sprout shifts its attention away from protecting itself and throws itself into the growth process instead. As the sprout's defenses weaken, its nutrients become more available to us. Several vitamins and fibers also increase in quantity— it's impressive and almost magical that a seed containing no vitamin C whatsoever suddenly has quite a lot of it after a few days' sprouting.

Sprouts and shoots can be grown year-round, which makes them even better. They don't care what season it is when grown at regular room temperature. What about light? Sprouts couldn't care less about light. In fact, they thrive in the dark. This makes sense when you think about where they

would sprout if they had any say in the matter—in the ground.

Remember, though, that shoots need a small amount of light.

Whether you have a south-facing porch or a tiny, north-facing window, you will be able to harvest microgreens. Shoots are clever and know how to make the best use of whatever light is available. A lush geranium will pitch a fit if situated to the north, but shoots hardly bat an eye. If they're placed within a reasonable distance of a window, you'll be able to start harvesting chlorophyll-rich microgreens after a week or two.

Being able to snip some twisty pea shoots straight into the salad bowl on a dark December evening is awesome, as is watching the snow fall outside your window as you sprinkle your breakfast sandwich liberally with freshly harvested broccoli shoots.

Sprouts and shoots are very budget friendly. Dried peas, beans, and lentils don't cost much, and neither do buckwheat, sunflower, and alfalfa seeds.

When seeds sprout, their volume increases: 3⅓ fluid ounces (1 dl) of dried peas turn into about 3 cups (7 dl) of sprouts. The champion producer—alfalfa—generates even more sprouts.

A pack of arugula, broccoli, or radish seeds might seem a bit pricey at first, but when you think of how far they will go, your salad ends up being a good buy. Two tablespoons of seeds produce a full tray of luscious shoots.

I suppose we hardly need to mention that sprouts and shoots are also great food if you care for the environment. Transporting dry seeds to the store is a smart use of energy. Once in the house, water is the only thing needed. The harvest ends up directly on your plate. So, if you like locally sourced food, you will love homegrown food!

Mung beans not only produce tasty sprouts, but also perky shoots.

FROM MIRACLE FOOD TO VIABLE WAR RATION—A HISTORY OF SPROUTING

When we seek out traditional recipes that feature sprouts, we very quickly find ourselves in Asia. It's not surprising then to find out that sprouts, as a food, have their origins there.

Soy sprouts are mentioned in Chinese texts as far back as 200 A.D., at which time dried sprouts were used medicinally. At the end of the sixteenth century, the Chinese physician Li Shih-Chen wrote in a famous medical treatise that sprouts can reduce inflammation, be used as a laxative, alleviate rheumatism, and build up the body.

Plenty of documentation from the beginning of the 1900s show that sprouts were sold in the Chinese markets. They were a vital source of food in the winter, especially in the colder, northern regions of China, when there were few other vegetables available.

We don't traditionally eat sprouts in the West, but there's been brisk work in sprouting as part of the production of beer and spirits. Barley grains are soaked and sprouted to produce malt. During the process, barley enzymes convert starch to malt sugar. Malt has also been used in bread baking and for brewing specific drinks such as the Swedish Christmas beverage called Julmust.

In the West, sprouting has played its part in the fight against scurvy. This disease was the scourge of the maritime population, who were at sea for months at a time. As many as half the seamen on the ships experienced periodontitis (tooth loss), muscle atrophy, and eventually death. It took a long time to discover that the cause of scurvy was a lack of vitamin C. In the latter part of the 1700s, the famous British explorer James Cook tried many different remedies during his travels to try to combat the problem, and he eventually succeeded. Among other things, sprouted wheat grain appeared to have beneficial effects during the early stages of scurvy. As it sprouts, wheat develops vitamin C.

In the United States, interest in sprouting took off during World War II. The worry was that, just like in Europe, combat would restrict the availability of meat and dairy products; this led to an intensified search for alternative sources of protein. In the end, the option that scientists came up with was sprouted seeds, grains, and beans, especially soybeans. The government went all out printing and distributing leaflets all over America on how to sprout and how to prepare dishes with sprouts. However, the protein shortage never occurred, and when the war ended in 1945, most people put those leaflets away.

In the mid-1960s, however, sprouting was back on the scene. Contributing to this renewed interest

<< *Adzuki beans, red lentils, and mung beans grown in a sprouting tower.*

was the back-to-the-land movement, the trend in DIY, heightened environmental awareness, and an enthusiasm for vegetarian foods. At the end of the decade, Ann Wigmore founded her first health institute in the United States and promoted her philosophy of "living foods." She can be considered the forerunner of today's raw food movement. Sprouts and shoots were a vital part of Wigmore's message on how to eat to boost your health.

This interest is very much alive in today's raw food trend. Soaking and sprouting is of course a smart way to make nutrients accessible to even those who prefer not to heat their food.

Lately, a focus on green shoots—or *microgreens*, to use the more familiar term—has emerged. Professional chefs were the first to discover and make use of these microvegetables, mostly for aesthetic purposes. A few pea shoots or teeny-tiny arugula leaves brightens up any dish.

Then the trend of urban gardening took root, with its message that no matter how small the plot, or how crowded the apartment, or how tiny the window, you can always grow something. Why not a few microgreen shoots?

Dried corn kernels produce pink-green sprouts that taste intensely sweet.

FROM SEED TO SPROUT—WHAT HAPPENS TO THE NUTRIENTS?

Seeds are little nutrition bombs packed with proteins, fiber, and minerals. The trouble is that they don't give up their nutrients readily. Inside the seed is a built-in plan to grow into a big, strong plant, so to be consumed as early as the seed stage would be a real blow to its pride. The nutrients are bound up through smart mechanisms that make it difficult for humans to get at them. However, by soaking and sprouting, we can fool the seed into believing that the coast is clear, which is not too good for the seed, but great for us. The seed opens and begins to grow. Its nutrient levels rise and become more available. Substances within the seed that protect it from, say, insects (and can, by the same token, be bad for us), start to break down.

Enzymes

In nature, a seed is dormant until it comes into contact with water. All the enzymes required to launch life's processes "sleep" inside the seed. Simply put, enzymes are substances that enable and accelerate chemical reactions. Once the seed is in water—and the temperature is right—it directs all its energy toward growing into a plant. The resting enzymes come alive. These enzymes, along with newer ones created during sprouting, make the nutrients in the seed more accessible.

Proteins, Fats, and Carbohydrates

The energy in the seed is stored as protein, fat, and carbohydrates. In chia, sunflower, and sesame seeds, fat is the dominant nutrient—it constitutes up to half the seeds' contents. However, legume seeds like yellow peas, lentils, and mung beans only have about 1 percent fat. Instead, they contain more carbohydrates, as do grain like seeds such as quinoa and buckwheat. The protein content in seeds is usually between 10 and 25 percent, with legume seeds topping the list. While sprouting, the total calorie count decreases, because the process requires, of course, a lot of energy. Carbohydrates break down into simple sugars, which in turn are quickly absorbed by the blood; you would think, therefore, that this would induce a high blood glucose response—(high GI—Glycemic Index). However, the few studies that have been conducted show the opposite: that in fact the blood glucose response is better, i.e., it produces a lower GI. The reason for this is probably due to the increase of phenolic compounds (see Protective Substances, p. 19) and soluble fibers (see Fiber, p. 16) that happens during sprouting.

Proteins are broken down into amino acids.

The fat content of sprouted seed decreases; the amount of fat that gets used up depends on how long you sprout the seed. Contrast a sunflower seed, which has half its energy in the form of fat, with, say, an almost fat-free sunflower shoot.

Vitamins

The quantity of several vitamins increases during sprouting. Vitamin B, including riboflavin and folate (folic acid is the synthetically derived folate found in nutritional supplements), have been shown to rise substantially. While most foods contain small amounts of riboflavin, it is found primarily in meat. This vitamin assists in breaking down carbohydrates, fats, and proteins.

Folate helps create new cells and red blood corpuscles. This vitamin is especially important during body growth and pregnancy.

Even levels of vitamin A increase when sprouts are growing. More accurately, it is carotene that gets a boost. Carotene is a substance the body can convert to vitamin A. It is vital to the proper functioning of our eyesight, skin, and mucous membranes. It is also critical to the development of the fetus.

As for vitamin C, most seeds don't have any to begin with, but it develops during sprouting. In research focusing on buckwheat and quinoa seeds, which do not contain any vitamin C at all, it was shown that after two to three days of sprouting, the level of vitamin C reached 24 milligrams and 7 milligrams per 3½ ounces (100 g) of sprouts, respectively. For reference, the recommended daily amount of vitamin C is 75 milligrams. This vitamin acts as an antioxidant in the body and helps build up cartilage and bone tissue. Even levels of vitamin E rise during sprouting. This vitamin acts as an antioxidant and protects our body tissues, among other things.

However, sprouts can't provide us with much in the way of vitamin B12. This is a vitamin that we need to acquire from the animal kingdom. Vegans need to take special care to get supplemental vitamin B12. The misunderstanding that sprouts are rich in vitamin B12 probably stems from the fact that bacteria produce this vitamin, and bacteria can grow on sprouts (see p. 20). But this is not something we want to have happen, because we then run the risk of levels of toxic bacteria rising, too.

Minerals

Seeds contain several types of minerals such as iron, magnesium, zinc, and calcium, and they're greedily protective of them. Phytic acid binds the minerals to the seeds and makes it difficult for us to absorb the minerals when we eat the seeds. During sprouting, phosphorus is released by the phytic acid molecule to supply the growing seed's need for phosphorus. The more phosphorus is released, the looser the phytic acid's grip on the other minerals. So now the minerals become easier for the plant to use, and easier for us to absorb as we eat the sprouts!

Minerals help with many different types of processes in the body. While we don't need large amounts of them, they're still vital to us.

Fiber

Dietary fiber is mainly found in vegetables, and we usually distinguish between soluble and insoluble fiber. Simply put, soluble fiber is fiber that is soluble in water and forms a gel; think about how oats behave when we make oatmeal, or what happens when flaxseeds are mixed with warm water. The pectin in fruit and berries is another example of soluble fiber.

An example of insoluble fiber is the shell surrounding different types of seeds. Soluble and insoluble fiber can coexist in varying amounts within the same food.

Through sprouting, the amount of soluble fiber increases somewhat, while the amount of insoluble decreases. On the whole, the level of fiber rises.

>> *Quick sprouts! Red lentils grow into a crisp tangle in only two to four days.*

Both soluble and insoluble fiber impart volume to food. Soluble fiber provides a good sense of satiety because its nutrients are absorbed more slowly by the body, which keeps blood glucose levels lower (lower GI). Insoluble fiber acts down lower in the gut, where it puts the intestines to work.

Gas-producing Substances

Legumes such as beans, lentils, and peas contain substances that can cause bouts of intestinal distress and gas. These substances are called oligosaccharides, and they are a type of carbohydrate that our digestive enzymes have trouble dealing with. Instead, they make a beeline to the colon. Down there, the colon's bacteria greet them with open arms and feast on them happily. In gratitude, those substances produce methane gas, carbon dioxide, and sulfur—in other words, farts.

It's typically recommended to soak seeds and beans in water and to change the water a few times to minimize the formation of gas. Sprouting decreases these substances further. After the seeds and beans have sprouted for two to six days, almost all those gas-producing substances will have disappeared.

Protective substances

Antioxidants is a collective term for substances that help protect the body against cell damage and fat oxidation. When seeds are sprouted, the number of antioxidants can increase enormously—up to 2,000 percent. This is partly because the number of vitamins increases. Vitamin C, E, and carotene (the precursor to vitamin A) are considered antioxidants. It's also a result of the larger amount of phenols, also known as *phenolics*. Phenolics are substances found in all vegetables and they provide taste, smell, and color. Their main purpose is to protect the plant from being eaten. Phenolics are considered

<< *Let sprouted lentils grow into green shoots.*

beneficial in the fight against cardiovascular disease, cancer, diabetes, and allergies, due to their anti-inflammatory, antioxidant, blood sugar, and cholesterol-lowering properties.

As mentioned before, seeds do their utmost not to be eaten by, say, insects. Lectins are protective substances found primarily in raw beans. Lectins can make it difficult for us to absorb protein, among other things. Very high doses of lectins can cause nausea, stomach pain, and in more serious cases, food poisoning. Kidney beans and runner beans contain a lot of lectins, as do brown, white, and black beans. Luckily, these substances are sensitive to heat and disappear with cooking. Sprouting also affects lectins, and the longer the tails are left to grow, the fewer lectins they will contain. But you still always need to cook sprouts from the above-mentioned seeds and beans.

Lectin levels are low in lentils, yellow and green peas, chickpeas, mung, and adzuki beans, which is why their sprouts do not need to be heated—not to get rid of lectins, in any case. You may still want to cook some of them anyway, at least for flavor.

The soybean is sort of in a class all by itself. It's not that it contains a lot of lectins (it doesn't); however, it does contain a lot of trypsin inhibitors, a group of substances that can also inhibit the absorption of nutrients. Trypsin inhibitors are reduced by sprouting, but make it a habit to cook soy sprouts for at least 15 minutes anyway.

Some seeds make use of saponins, another type of protective compound. They are located on the exterior of quinoa and millet husks, for example. Saponins impart a bitter taste but are easy to remove by rinsing the seeds thoroughly in water. Today, it is often done by the manufacturer before sale. It's easy to see if there are saponins on the seeds because they will foam when the seeds are rinsed. Saponins are even an ingredient in soap and washing products. *Sapo* is the Latin name for soap.

If you sprout any other seeds than those described in this book, make sure to find out what is relevant for those specific seeds, about lectins, and about specific preparation.

From Sprout to Shoot

A new process begins once sprouts have grown into shoots and are placed in the light. The sun's rays help the shoots convert water and the air's carbon dioxide into energy-rich carbohydrates and oxygen. The stalk and the tiny leaves begin to turn green. The rate at which this happens is fascinating; just watch the shoots for half an hour and see how they change color. That's chlorophyll being created, and the chlorophyll cells are the engine for creating new energy. This energy can be stored as carbohydrates and then be used for growth. Shoots, just like vegetables and fruit, contain protective substances in the form of vitamin C and other antioxidants. The few studies that have been conducted have shown that shoots typically contain a higher concentration of healthy nutrients than their fully grown vegetable counterparts. But we must take into consideration the amount of shoots we can eat. They are light and airy and often have quite a strong flavor. It is probably far easier to eat 3½ ounces (100g) of radishes—about 10 of them—than to consume the equivalent weight in radish shoots.

We are still only familiar with a tiny fraction of the thousands of substances affecting our health that are in foods of the vegetable world. Without exaggerating the importance of sprouts and shoots, we can assert that they are a good source of antioxidants and other protective substances.

Safe Handling

Sprouts and shoots grow best where it's humid and at room temperature. Unfortunately, bacteria and mold also thrive under those conditions. It is important to deal with sprouts and shoots safely. Always wash your hands before handling seeds and

growing sprouts; in fact, try touching them as little as possible.

Always rinse the seeds thoroughly before sprouting. Remove damaged seeds, small stones, and other debris. Also, rinse them thoroughly after soaking. Even then, keep an eye out for seeds that look different. Maybe they didn't swell like the others, or maybe they have a different color. If that's the case, throw them away. They might turn and infect neighboring sprouting seeds. Take great care every time you rinse the sprouts during sprouting. Use cold water.

Utensils used for sprouting must be spotlessly clean. Wash the utensils after using them, preferably in a dishwasher set at its highest temperature. Or dry them for approximately a quarter of an hour in an oven preheated to 212°F (100°C).

Whether growing in soil or on paper, it's important that things don't get too wet, otherwise mold will grow. Also, keep a close eye during warm summer days or if there is inadequate ventilation. However, keep in mind that several types of shoots develop mini-roots at the sprouting stage, and this white fuzz can easily be mistaken for white mold. This is relevant for radish, sunflower, broccoli, and mustard shoots, among other things.

Sprouts and shoots that are ready should be stored loosely wrapped in the refrigerator; leave the packaging slightly open to allow for enough air circulation. And of course, eat the sprouts as soon as possible. It's difficult to gauge how long they will keep in the refrigerator, so use your senses. Do the sprouts look nice and fresh? Do they smell okay? Finally, do they taste right?

If you're unsure, you're better off preparing the sprouts and shoots by cooking, sautéing, or deep-frying them. Heat kills bacteria at around 158°F (70°C).

Most bacteria found on sprouts are harmless to humans. However, outbreaks where sprouts were suspected of being the culprit have occurred several times. Commercially grown sprouts have carried salmonella or EHEC (Enterohemorrhagic Escherichia Coli) strains of bacteria; the bacteria is transmitted by sprouts rinsed in dirty water or via the original seeds.

Some producers, such as those in Sweden, pasteurize or treat seeds with hydrogen peroxide before they are sprouted to avoid the growth of dangerous bacteria. You can pasteurize some seeds yourself at home if you want to feel extra safe.

Pasteurizing at Home

Pasteurizing seeds before they sprout guarantees that any potential bacteria on the seeds' surface will be destroyed. You can do this very simply by submerging the seeds in hot water for 30 seconds.

Large seeds such as mung beans and chickpeas are not harmed by pasteurizing. Hot water will kill any lurking bacteria without letting the heat penetrate and compromise the viability of the seed.

Small seeds are more sensitive, so you may not succeed in heating them without also hampering their ability to germinate. Certain small seeds will also produce a gel when they come into contact with water

(chia, arugula, and mustard seeds, for example), so they are not good candidates for pasteurization.

How to pasteurize:

1. Bring water to boil in a large saucepan.

2. Pull the saucepan off the heat once the water is boiling. Put a thermometer in the water.

3. Pour ice cold water into a large bowl.

4. Transfer the seeds to a sieve. Rinse them thoroughly under cold running water.

5. When the thermometer registers 176°F–185°F (80°C–85°C), lower the sieve with the seeds into the water for 30 seconds. Stir the seeds to make sure they all come in contact with the water.

6. Remove the sieve with the seeds. Transfer the seeds directly into the ice-cold water. Stir the seeds so they all cool down immediately. Let them sit in the cold water for 5 minutes.

7. Transfer the seeds back into the sieve and let them drain. They are now ready to grow into sprouts or shoots.

Sprouting buckwheat in a sieve is very convenient.

SPROUTS

Sprouting is easy and super-fast. All you need is a colander, sieve, or a large glass jar. Soak a handful of seeds and you're on your way! Enjoy the sprouts plain, mix them into smoothies, bake them into bread, fry them in falafel, or shape them into luscious coconut and coffee truffles.

Sprouts are just the ticket for those who have no patience but who still enjoy growing things. If we even can call it growing . . . Soaking, followed by rinsing for a few days, is all that's required. But it's fun—the seeds germinate, and it's fast!

Unlike with shoots, with sprouts you eat the entire seed, including the grown-out tail. Shoots are left to grow a stalk and leaves.

Most of the seeds I've selected belong to the legume family. That's because lentils, beans, and peas are so simple to sprout, so tasty, so satisfying, and are suited to cooking; they're not only good for garnish. Even quinoa, buckwheat, and sunflower seeds are quick-growing favorites.

Soaking

Most seeds like to soak for a bit, some a little longer than others, to wake up from dormancy. The seeds absorb water, swell, and prepare themselves for sprouting.

Start by rinsing the seeds in a colander (or in a fine-mesh sieve, if the seeds are small) to remove any dust and dirt. Transfer the seeds to a basin, bowl, or jar, and fill it with cold water. Fill the vessel with plenty of water—at least three times the volume of seed—because it's amazing how much water some seeds can take in. As a rule, small seeds require less soaking time. On the other hand, large seeds, like beans and peas, need several hours to wake up. Even better, they can soak up to twenty-four hours. For simplicity's sake, I let all seeds, large and small, soak overnight. You don't need to worry that some seeds won't survive a full night's soak.

Make a habit of checking the soaked seeds thoroughly, and remove any that didn't swell and stayed their original size. Discard any seeds that are discolored or damaged, as they will not sprout.

Some seeds such as arugula, chia, and cress form a gel around the seed when they come into contact with water. This makes them challenging to soak; since they turn into a large, jellified mass, they're also hard to handle. These seeds are more easily sprouted directly without soaking, but read more about them on p. 89, since they're more suitable as shoots.

Sprouting

After the seeds have soaked, it's time for them to sprout. Regardless of how you choose to do it, the most important thing is to make sure the seeds are constantly moist. Why not just leave them soaking, then? you might ask. Well, it isn't quite that simple. Once the soaked seed's outer shell or hull has begun to open, the seed will need not only water but also oxygen to survive. Humidity is vital, and the seeds are at their most delicate at the onset of the process. If you let them dry out completely once they've begun growing, nothing can get them going again. You'll have to start all over again with new seeds.

Begin by pouring off the soaking water. Rinse the seeds thoroughly, moving them around with clean hands so the water reaches everywhere. Throw away the seeds that are split in half, damaged, or discolored. Then, sprout the seeds according to your chosen method. A good rule of thumb is to rinse the seeds twice every twenty-four hours, morning and evening being the easiest times to remember. If you can do more, your sprouts will thank you for an extra rinse or two. And if you know that a longer stretch of time will go by before you can rinse them again, place a plastic bag over the growing container (without sealing it completely) to capture the moisture a little longer.

As a rule, the sprouts will grow quicker if the environment is slightly warmer than if it is cold.

All the sprouting in this book was done at regular room temperature, between 66.2°F and 71.6°F

>> *Dormant enzymes wake up when the mung beans are soaked in water.*

(19°C–22°C). I find it most convenient to keep the sprouts on the kitchen counter near the sink. If there's an area in your home that's slightly warmer, you can always try to leave the sprouting container there to hasten the sprouting process a bit. During wintertime, for example, a spot by the window might be too cold; it's better to try someplace warmer.

Traditional advice says to let the sprouting take place in the dark. This is to mimic the seed's real life where it would sprout under the soil's surface. If the sprouts are exposed to light, the photosynthesis begins and the sprouts funnel more of their energy into starch and cellulose. But there is, of course, a slight difference between a seed that needs to gather its strength and courage before pushing up and through earth to develop into a strong plant, and a sprout that goes all out for two or three days and then, quite simply, gets eaten. So you do not need to heed the advice of placing your sprouts in a dark cupboard or pantry too seriously.

If you use an open container, such as a colander or a sieve, you just need to cover it with a kitchen towel, a large plate, or a saucepan lid so you also keep out dirt and dust. This step is especially important if you keep sprouts by the sink—that way they're protected from splashing dish-washers. Sprouting seeds don't thrive at all on showers of dishwashing liquid—it can hamper their growth.

Regardless of sprouting method, I've noticed the outcome is more or less the same whether you sprout in regular, indirect household daylight or in total darkness. However, avoid placing sprouts in direct sunlight, not just because it might be too hot, but because the sprouts also run the risk of drying out.

Methods

There are several different ways to sprout, from the classic jar method to sprouting in a cloth bag. All methods boil down to the same principle: the sprouts must be easy to rinse and drain thoroughly.

The container shouldn't close completely, because the sprouts thrive with proper air circulation.

The method you choose will depend on your personal preferences. Sprouting in a colander or sieve is convenient if you're only going to sprout a large batch of one type of seed, such as dried yellow peas or mung beans for a falafel. However, a multilevel growing tower will work better if you want to sprout several different types of seeds simultaneously. Hardcore sprouters like to fill a dish rack with large jars so they have a whole gang of different varieties going at once.

Colander/Sieve

This is an incredibly simple method, especially if you're going for a larger batch of one type of seed, or—why not—for two or several kinds; it all depends on how many colanders/sieves you can spare for a few days. Choose a colander or sieve that's made of stainless steel or plastic. Zinc, iron, and aluminum might react with the constant moisture and then discolor the sprouts and make them taste bad. I won't claim that metals are absorbed by the sprouts, but choose stainless steel to be on the safe side.

Transfer the soaked seeds to a colander (or a fine-mesh sieve, if the seeds are small) and rinse them thoroughly with cold water. Then leave the seeds in the colander for the duration of the sprouting process. It's easy to rinse them that way. The colander's holes help with air circulation, which in turn prevents mold or bacteria from taking hold. Keep the colander over a big bowl to let the water drain properly. Cover the colander with a saucepan lid or a kitchen towel. Rinse carefully at least twice every twenty-four hours. Soon you'll notice the small tails creeping down through the colander's holes. Don't turn the sprouts over or shake them too vigorously while rinsing because the tails can break off and ruin the sprouts.

Do you wonder how sprouts cope with being stacked on top of each other? Remember how a seed develops in soil? Talk about pressure! Sprouts are used to putting up a fight; a little resistance won't do them any harm. In some commercial productions, mung beans are grown under pressure, which makes them extra springy and crisp.

Glass Jar and Cheesecloth

This is the classic method. And yes—it works great. You can buy a growing jar with a special mesh-gridded lid and a contraption to put the jar on so that it leans and makes the water drain off properly. Or you can use a simple, larger jar and place at an angle on the dish rack; it works just as well. Put a piece of cheesecloth over the opening and secure it with a rubber band. Or why not find a nice piece of lace curtain in a thrift store, wash it, and cut it to size? The most important thing is that the fabric be loosely woven to allow the water to drain off freely. Choose a jar that doesn't taper at the top, since a wide opening makes it easier to remove the sprouts when they're done growing. Remember that seeds increase vastly in size—a tablespoon of alfalfa seed turns into several cups of sprouts.

Use a totally clean jar, and make sure no dishwashing liquid residue is left in it that could disturb the sprouting process. Rinse the seeds thoroughly and put them in the jar. Cover them with cold water (at least three times the seeds' volume) and let them soak. Cover the jar's opening with a piece of loosely woven fabric, and secure it with a rubber band. Now it's easy to rinse the sprouts— which you should do several times immediately. Place the jar in a stand, in a dish rack, or in a deep bowl with the opening pointed downward to let all the excess water drain. By all means, cover the jar with a kitchen towel. Rinse thoroughly at least twice daily until the sprouts are ready. The sprouts can stay in the jar while being stored in the refrigerator. Leave the jar upside down in a deep basin or bowl in the refrigerator, and rinse the sprouts every other or every third day. This will help them stay fresh longer. The cold doesn't encourage further growth.

Sprouting Kits

There are different sprouting kits, even boxes, available in stores. The most common types have two or three levels made of pierced, rimmed plastic trays. They work on the same principle as the colander method: the sprouts are easy to rinse, and the excess water drains into the collection tray at the bottom. The air circulates freely between the levels through the holes. This minimizes the risk of mold and bacterial growth.

A tower construction is smart, because you can have several types of sprouts and shoots growing at the same time. But if you want to grow larger batches, this setup might feel a bit on the small side.

There are also terracotta growing kits, but they're smaller than their plastic counterparts and are best suited to those wanting to sprout in small amounts.

Growing Bag

This method comes highly recommended by the many who have tried it. I am not entirely convinced—not yet, anyway. The seeds are placed in a bag made of linen or hemp; there are also bags made from synthetic materials. These bags are sold at some health food stores and online. You can easily make your own bag, too. The entire bag is submerged in water at the time of rinsing and then hung up or placed on a dish rack. All water drains off and the air can circulate freely through the fabric.

Full speed ahead with sprouts and shoots! Glass jar, colander, sieve, and cloth bag are best for sprouts. Plastic and terracotta stands and towers work for both sprouts and shoots. The plastic tray with the black grid is for growing in water and is used primarily to produce shoots (read more about this on p. 91).

SPROUTING IN A COLANDER—STEP BY STEP

1. Pour the seeds into a colander. Rinse them thoroughly with cold water over a bowl or directly under the tap.

2. Transfer the seeds to a bowl or a jar. Soak them in plenty of water; check the timetable for each type of seed.

3. Put the soaked seeds back into the colander. Pick over them and throw out all damaged and discolored seeds.

4. Rinse the seeds thoroughly once again.

5. Cover the bowl with a towel, a plate, or the lid of a saucepan.

6. Rinse the sprouts at least twice daily.

7. Rinse the sprouts when they're ready, and let them drain well.

8. Remove any pieces of seed husk you spot with a slotted spoon or a skimmer. (See more in the section How to Harvest on p. 31).

How to Harvest

The time at which sprouts are ready to eat can range from just one day to about five or six days. A shorter "tail" makes for a denser sprout, while longer tails give crisper, lighter sprouts. Get to know them by tasting them now and then as they grow. Certain sprouts, such as buckwheat, quinoa, and hulled sunflower seeds, are ready in a day or two; they do not improve by sprouting any longer. Others, like mung beans and lentils, can be eaten either short or long-tailed, depending on your preference. Use the sprouting table shown by each sprout as a guide.

Once the sprouts are ready, rinse them thoroughly one last time and drain them well. If they've been growing in a colander (or in a sprouter), pull them up carefully and loosen the sprout tails that have grown through the holes of the colander. Most beans, lentils, and peas have a soft outer hull that cracks and falls off once the legumes begin to grow. To remove this shell or not is purely a question of aesthetics. Personally, I don't think the shells are unsightly—sometimes quite the opposite in fact; the mung beans' green hull makes a pretty addition to any salad or stir-fry. And it doesn't matter if there are hulls in falafels or smoothies since the sprouts are mixed in or pureed anyway. You'll get some extra fiber as a bonus.

All the same, if you prefer to remove the hulls, here's how to do it: Put the sprouts in a large bowl, pot, or basin. Fill it with enough water so that the sprouts are separated and moving around freely. Stir the water with a skimmer or a slotted spoon to create a whirlpool in the water to push the sprouts around in. Typically, the hulls will come off the sprouts and float to the water's surface but some might sink to the bottom. Using the skimmer or a spoon, quickly fish out the hulls that float to the surface. Repeat this process until most of the hulls have been removed. If you don't have a skimmer or a slotted spoon, stir the water with a regular spoon or a ladle. Quickly but carefully pour off most of the water into the sink and hopefully most of the hulls will leave the pot with the water. Fill up the pot with water and repeat the process a few more times.

Let the sprouts drain thoroughly in a colander.

How to Store

If the sprouts are not eaten immediately, they must be stored in the refrigerator. They will continue to grow, but the cooler environment will slow down the process significantly. Make sure that the sprouts are completely drained of water before storing them; it's not good for them to stand in water.

If you've used a jar for sprouting, by all means store the sprouts in that jar in the refrigerator, and leave it in the same position (i.e., with the opening pointing down) in a bowl. A plastic bag or plastic jar is also good for storing sprouts. Just remember not to close the opening completely because sprouts like to breathe. Do the sprouts look droopy? If so, rinse them in cold water and let them drain thoroughly.

How long sprouts stay fresh depends on a lot of things, like how long they sprouted, the temperature in which they sprouted, and the temperature inside your fridge. And maybe most importantly, if they were handled using safe and sanitary practices. I recommend you use your sense of smell and taste to decide if the sprouts are edible. Do they smell and look fresh? Do they taste as they should? If you're unsure, heat the sprouts before you use them. Any bacteria will die at 158°F (70°C).

SPROUT PROFILES

ADZUKI BEANS (red mung bean)

In Asia, cooked adzuki beans are often used in sweet cakes and other baked goods. Adzukis, or adukis, as the beans are also called, make very pretty sprouts. The lilac-brown shell cracks open as the sprout continues to grow. The adzuki is a relative of the mung bean, but it doesn't sprout as quickly as its cousin.

SUITABLE FOR

Just like mung bean sprouts, adzukis work well fried in pad thai or vegetable stir-fry. Or add them to a stew. They are chewier than mung and lentil sprouts, so they're better eaten cooked than raw. If you still wish to eat them raw, wait until the tail is a little longer, which makes them tastier. But don't let them get too long because that makes them stringy and unappetizing.

WHERE TO FIND THEM

Most well-stocked grocery stores will carry dried adzuki beans. The germination rate can vary between different producers. Try different types until you find the one you like best.

METHOD

All methods discussed work. A colander or large jar works for bigger batches.

HOW TO

Pick your method. Rinse once more, preferably—not just morning and night. In my experience, adzuki beans are more prone to drying out than other legume seeds. The sprouts will be ready after three to five days. You can, of course, remove the lilac-brown outer hull as per the method described on p. 31, but I personally feel that it is just this hull that makes the sprouts so lovely.

Soak time: At least 12 hours. 24 hours is better.
Sprouting time after soaking: 72 to 120 hours
Sprout yield: Adzuki beans: approx. 1¾ oz (50 g) or 3⅓ fl oz (1 dl) will yield approximately 10½ oz (300 g) or 2½ cups (6 dl) of sprouts.

ALFALFA SEEDS

Along with mung beans, alfalfa seeds are probably what we associate most often with sprouting. It's easy to understand why: one single tablespoon of these mini seeds quickly and reliably produces a truly big, crisp, and fresh bundle of sprouts.

SUITABLE FOR

Alfalfa belongs to the legume family, and the sprouts do indeed taste a bit like peas. The thin sprouts are best raw and are not improved by heating. Sprinkle some sprouts over your sandwich, let them crisp up a wrap, or top your salads with them. But don't mix them with salad dressing ahead of time because the delicate sprouts won't stand up to it. Their mild flavor goes very well in smoothies or chilled soups.

WHERE TO FIND THEM

Alfalfa seeds are primarily used for sprouting, so it is almost impossible not to find them. The seeds are sold at well-stocked grocery stores, health food stores, and online.

METHOD

The best way is to use a jar, which keeps moisture levels even. If the thin sprouts start to dry out, they quickly lose their crispness. Remember to use a large jar, because the seeds increase surprisingly in volume. Kept in a sieve, the sprouts will pull downward, so if you want the classic snarl of alfalfa sprouts, go for the jar method.

HOW TO

Follow the jar method. The sprouts will be ready after three to five days. If you want sprouts with snazzy green tops, place the jar on a windowsill from the third day on. It's fascinating to see how quickly chlorophyll is created; it only takes an hour or two for the color to change from pale yellow to green.

The sprouts will keep best if they are kept in the refrigerator, in the same conditions as while they were sprouting, i.e., in a jar tipped upside down in a bowl or basin.

<< Adzuki – an extra nice sprout.

Rinse them every other day or every third day, and they will stay fresh.

Soak time: At least 6 hours, but preferably overnight.
Sprouting time after soaking: 72 to 120 hours
Yield: Alfalfa seeds: approx. 0.42 oz (12 g) or 1 tbsp will yield 2.46 oz (70 g) or approx. 2 cups (5 dl) of sprouts.

BUCKWHEAT

A great little seed for novices! Buckwheat pays off immediately, as it only takes twenty-four hours to witness the first pretty little tails emerge. While it's easy to believe that buckwheat is related to wheat, buckwheat is an herb that's not related to wheat grain at all, and that makes it totally gluten-free, too.

You'll find the pigment fagopyrin on the exterior of the buckwheat seed. In very large quantities, it's an irritant to eyes and skin. To remove the fagopyrin, you must rinse the seeds in hot water before you sprout them.

SUITABLE FOR
Sprouted buckwheat has a very pleasant, nutty flavor. Mix the sprouts with water, coconut, or oat mylk to make a raw muesli, or cook it like normal oatmeal. The seeds are also tasty baked in bread. Or toast them in the oven on low heat for a crisp, crunchy treat. The sprouts make a good base for vegetarian burgers, too—they add a nice chewiness. Or toss a handful of sprouts into a salad.

WHERE TO FIND THEM
Choose whole buckwheat seeds for sprouting. Grocery stores also sell

crushed buckwheat or buckwheat flakes, but these are processed and will not sprout. Neither will the roasted seeds. Whole buckwheat sold at grocery stores has usually been hulled, and that's the type you'll want to use.

Buckwheat is also sold nonhulled, with its hard, black shell left intact; that kind is not useful for sprouting. However, this variety is recommended for growing shoots. Now, there is an ongoing debate as to whether it's a good idea to eat buckwheat shoots in large quantities because it's primarily in the green parts—the stalk and leaves—where we find a lot of fagopyrin.

METHOD
All methods discussed work, but the most practical way is to use a colander.

HOW TO
Regardless of the method you use, first place the buckwheat in a sieve or colander and rinse it under hot, running water for about thirty seconds. Then, rinse it immediately under cold water for about two minutes. Now, follow your chosen method. After soaking the seeds, rinse them thoroughly under cold, running water, and go over the seeds carefully to make sure that all the slippery gel-like coating on the seeds has been completely removed. Continue to rinse the seeds very carefully because new coating is generated as the seeds sprout.

After about forty-eight hours, or when the buckwheat grows tails about the same size as the seed itself, the buckwheat is ready to use.

Soak time: Approximately 8 hours, but up to 24 hours is fine.
Sprouting time after soaking:

About 48 hours.
Yield: Whole buckwheat seeds: approx. 2.82 oz (80 g) or 3⅓ fl oz (1 dl) will yield about 6 oz (170 g) or 8½ fl oz (2½ dl) of sprouts.

YELLOW PEAS—AND GREEN PEAS

A true superhero seed! Just picture how fast and easy our humble, low-cost soup peas can become cool sprouts. And you can turn them into good-looking green shoots if you like (but that's another story you can read about on p. 96). It seems almost too good to be true. You can, of course, make soup with the sprouts, too; the only difference from the classic version is that this one will cook faster and be gentler on your digestion.

SUITABLE FOR
With their nutlike sweetness, yellow peas can be incorporated into many dishes. In recipes that call for chickpeas, yellow peas work just as well (even better, if you ask me). Their sprouts only need to grow a small tail if they're to be mixed into burgers, falafel, soup, or a stew. Let them sprout for a few more days if you'd rather add them to a salad. They'll become light and crisp and even more digestible for your gut. But do go easy at first if you're not used to eating raw pea sprouts.

WHERE TO FIND THEM
Dried yellow peas can be found at any well-stocked grocery store. If you spy a bag of dried green peas next to them, grab it, too! They become lovely sprouts, and their mild green

coloring makes them really beautiful (read more about them below).

METHOD
All discussed methods work. For bigger batches, a colander and large jar methods work best.

HOW TO
Pick your method. Peas develop at different rates when they're soaked—some can be a little slow to start—so it's better to let them sit in water for a while, preferably about twenty-four hours if you can. This way you don't end up pulling out peas that might have sprouted had you given them just a bit more time. After twenty-four to forty-eight hours, most of the peas will have sprouted a small tail. Taste them as they grow.

If you have the energy and are so inclined, rinse the peas per the instructions on p. 31, as this will remove the outer hull. I never do this with peas, because I don't think the thin, translucent covering affects either their flavor or their looks.

Soak time: At least 12 hours, preferably 24.
Sprouting time after soaking:
72 to 120 hours
Yield: Yellow peas: approx. 2½ oz (75 g) or 3⅓ fl oz (1 dl) yields approx. 7 oz (200 g) or approx. 2 cups (4½ dl) sprouts.

GREEN PEAS

Dried green peas are also sold at grocery stores, but they're less common. That's a shame, and not just because they're so pretty with their matte, light-green coloring. These peas are a little sweeter than their yellow counterparts. Sprout them and use them as you would yellow peas. Their color will fade a little as sprouting progresses.

CHICKPEAS

A hearty pea that's great for sprouting. You can eat the sprouts raw, but frankly most people won't find it very appetizing that way. I believe they're much enhanced when prepared in some kind of dish. Raw chickpeas are a bit too crunchy.

SUITABLE FOR
You can use chickpea sprouts in any dish that calls for chickpeas. Just remember that cooking times will be shorter and that you will need a larger number of sprouted peas (which contain more water than those that have only been soaked). You can make falafel, hummus, spicy stews, and vegetarian burgers, or roast them in the oven or in a skillet with some oil and spices for a crunchy snack.

WHERE TO FIND THEM
Dried chickpeas can be found at most well-stocked grocery stores.

METHOD
All discussed methods work. For bigger batches, a colander or large jar works best.

HOW TO
Follow one of the methods discussed. Most of the chickpeas will have a small tail after about forty-eight hours of sprouting. How long you want them to sprout depends on your own taste preferences—test the sprouts to figure out the best length. If you want to remove the translucent hull that comes off the peas, follow the method on p. 31. To remove the hull is purely a question of aesthetics since it doesn't affect the flavor.

Soak time: At least 12 hours. Chickpeas can soak for up to 24 hours.
Sprouting time after soaking:
72 to 96 hours
Yield: Chickpeas: approx. 2¾ oz (80 g) or 3⅓ fl oz (1 dl) will yield approx. 7 oz (200 g) or 1¾ cups (4 dl) sprouts.

LENTILS

They come in red, green, and black, and are super easy to sprout! Their volume increases impressively: a little over 3 fl oz (1 dl) will turn into about 3½ cups (8 dl) of sprouts in just 3 to 4 days.

SUITABLE FOR
Lentils sprouts are mild-tasting and fit a lot of different occasions and dishes. You can use the sprouts as soon as twenty-four to forty-eight hours if you want to include them in soups or mix them into burgers. However, let the lentils sprout for a few more days if you wish to add them to a fresh salad, toss them into a stir-fry, or sprinkle them over a sandwich.

WHERE TO FIND THEM
All dried lentils work here, unless they've been precooked or processed in any other way. Red lentils are occasionally sold as "split lentils," i.e., shelled and cut in half to make them cook faster. They won't sprout well, if at all. The packaging will sometimes—but not always—say "split," so check the lentils carefully to confirm that they are whole.

Small, shiny, black lentils called Beluga lentils become especially

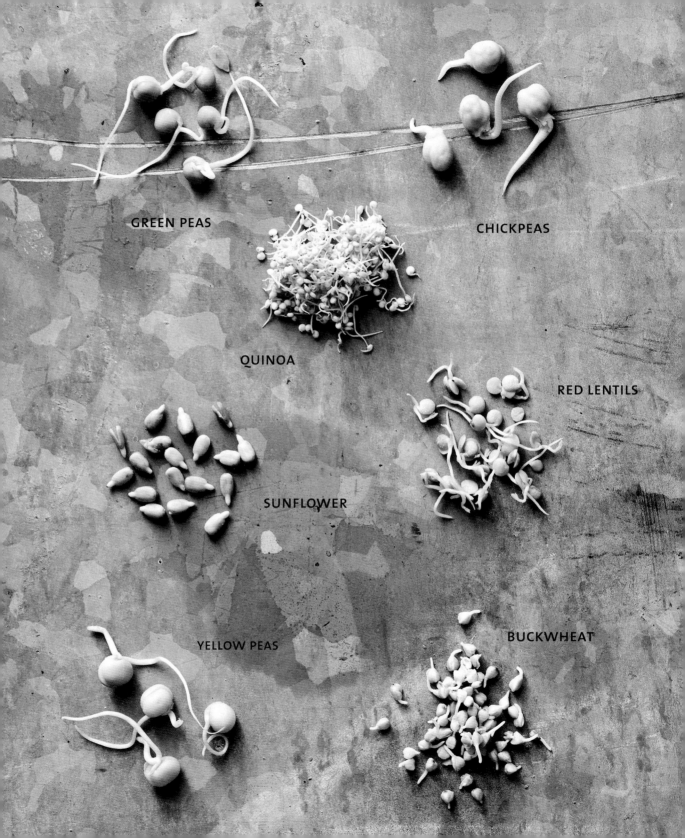

GREEN PEAS

CHICKPEAS

QUINOA

RED LENTILS

SUNFLOWER

YELLOW PEAS

BUCKWHEAT

ALFALFA

ADZUKI BEANS

SOYBEANS

MUNG BEANS

GREEN LENTILS

BLACK LENTILS

beautiful sprouts and are perfect in salads. Both regular green lentils and the more upmarket Puy lentils (which only come from the French area of the same name) grow willingly into sprouts.

METHOD

All discussed methods work. Be mindful of the size of the container; lentils increase considerably in volume.

HOW TO

Follow one of the discussed methods. Lentils sprout incredibly fast; after only a day, there's usually a split in the lentil with a sprout peeking out. Do a taste test to see when you feel they're ready. Shorter sprouting makes for a meatier sprout, while longer sprouting makes them crispier and fluffier.

Soak time: About 8 hours to overnight.
Sprouting time after soaking:
48 to 96 hours
Yield:
Black lentils: approx. 3 oz (90 g) or 3⅓ fl oz (1 dl) will yield approx. 10½ oz (300 g) or 3¾ cups (9 dl) of sprouts.

Green lentils: approx. 2¾ oz (80 g) or 3⅓ fl oz (1 dl) will yield approx. 8¾ oz (250 g) or 4¾ cups (11 dl) of sprouts.

Red lentils: approx. 2¾ oz (80 g) or 3⅓ fl oz (1 dl) will yield approx. 10½ oz (300 g) or 4¾ fl oz (11 dl) of sprouts.

MUNG BEANS

What we commonly refer to as bean sprouts, sold fresh or in cans, are just mung beans. It really is the ultimate sprout: quick, easy, and ever so useful! The green outer hull splits when the sprouts develop. You can remove it, of course, but I think it adds a rather beautiful touch.

SUITABLE FOR

These are very versatile sprouts. If you harvest them after just a day or two, you can sauté the fat, meaty sprouts in a little soy sauce or add them to a stir-fry like pad thai. Or cook them for a few minutes, then rinse and chill them and marinate them with other vegetables. Left to sprout a few days more, you'll end up with a crispy jumble of sprouts perfect for salads.

WHERE TO FIND THEM

It's difficult to go wrong here! Dried mung beans are . . . dried mung beans. They'll be with the dried beans, lentils, and peas.

METHOD

All discussed methods work. A colander or large jar works best for bigger batches.

HOW TO

Use the colander or the jar method. After sprouting for about twenty-four hours, the green outer hull will have split and a small tail will have emerged. Be careful toward the end when you rinse the sprouts: if you stir them too vigorously, the sprouts' tails at the bottom of the colander might break off.

When the sprouts are ready, rinse them one last time and let them drain. Pull sprouts that have grown in a colander straight up; most of them will loosen easier that way. Store the sprouts in the refrigerator. If you have the energy and are so inclined, rinse the sprouts according to the instructions on p. 31 to remove the green hull.

Soak time: 12 hours. Mung beans can soak for up to 24 hours.
Sprouting time after soaking:
48 to 120 hours
Yield: Mung beans: after 4 days, approx. 3¾ oz (110 g) or 3½ fl oz (1 dl) will yield approx. 14 oz (400 g) or 5 cups (12 dl) of sprouts.

EXTRA CRISPY—FOR EXTRA CREDIT

Mung beans that are available commercially will often have been cultivated using a pressure method. The beans are layered so they're kept under pressure from top to bottom. A weight is often placed on top to add extra pressure so the sprouts are forced to grow thicker to work against the weight. This gives them a crispier texture. Without this pressure, they would be longer and thinner.

If you'd like to try the same method, place the soaked beans in two layers on a single tray in a sprouting tower. Place the tray over the collection tray that comes with the tower. Put a plate or flat board that fits inside the sprouting tray on top of the sprouts. Add some weight–a heavy mortar or a stone–on top. Cover everything with a kitchen towel or a plastic bag. Remove the plate and weight at least twice every twenty-four hours and rinse.

SUNFLOWER SEEDS

Hulled sunflower seeds produce fine sprouts in only a day or two. They're ready when the tail is just emerging; all that's needed is the tiniest slip of an inch (a few millimeters).

Of course, it's tempting to let these seeds sprout for longer—it's so easy, after all! But resist because, when overgrown, the sprouts' pleasant, nutty flavor disappears and a nasty, bitter taste takes over. (However, the bitterness goes away again if you grow the sprouts into shoots. The shoots are nice and mild.)

SUITABLE FOR

These nut-flavored sprouts are great in breads, scones, and rolls. They provide good "chew" to salads, oatmeal, and chia puddings, as well as vegetarian burgers. Make your smoothie more satisfying by blending in a handful of sunflower sprouts. Or roast them with some salt or soy sauce for a snack.

WHERE TO FIND THEM

Choose plain seeds without hulls; don't buy them roasted or salted. Some packages contain many split and damaged sunflower seeds, which are not good for sprouting. The damaged seeds cannot sprout, so they risk going bad while the viable ones sprout. If you'd rather grow sunflower seeds into microgreens, it's safer to buy whole seeds in their shell (see p. 100).

METHOD

The colander method is the most practical way to go, even though you can use one of the other methods, too.

HOW TO

Use the recommended method. The time required for this seed's soaking and sprouting is limited. After twelve hours, the seed will have cracked and the tail will have begun to develop. The sprouts are ready when they are only a fraction of an inch long. Taste them often, because they turn bitter surprisingly fast; the flavor should be nice and nutty. After a few days, the sprouts might develop a brown tinge. This isn't dangerous; they react with the oxygen in the air the same way a peeled apple turns brown after being exposed to air. Sunflower sprouts taste best and have the best color immediately after being harvested, but they will keep for a few days in the refrigerator.

Soak time: At least 2 hours, but up to 24 hours will work, too.
Sprouting time after soaking: 24 to 48 hours
Yield: Sunflower seeds: approx. 2 oz (60 g) or 3⅓ fl oz (1 dl) will yield approx. 5 oz (140 g) or 1¼ cup (3 dl) of sprouts.

SOYBEANS

The soybean's protein content places it well above other legumes; it packs an impressive 34 percent. It also contains quite a lot of fat. Koreans have a long tradition of soy sprouting. I've noticed that during warm summer days, the sprouts can become discolored after three or four days. While this doesn't affect their flavor, they don't look very appealing. It's best to sprout soybeans during the colder time of the year.

SUITABLE FOR

Add the sprouts to salads and stews. Always cook soybean sprouts for at least 15 minutes; this will remove the trypsin inhibitors that can hamper the uptake of protein.

WHERE TO FIND THEM

Soybeans are available in grocery stores. Dried, they look like small, round peas. Once soaked, they take on an oval, beanlike shape. Their size can vary from small to large, and they can all be sprouted. Germination rates vary between sources, so try out a few.

METHOD

All the discussed methods work, but a colander works best here.

HOW TO

Choose the above method. It will take about five days for the sprouts to be ready. The longer they are left to sprout, the more tryptosin inhibitors are broken down. Tryptosin makes it difficult for the body to absorb the food's proteins, so always make sure to cook soybeans for at least 15 minutes before eating them, or before including them in a dish.

Soak time: At least 12 hours. Soybeans can soak for up to 24 hours.
Sprouting time after soaking: Approximately 120 hours
Yield: Soybeans: approx. 2½ oz (70 g) or 3⅓ fl oz (1dl) will yield approx. 14 oz (200 g) or 1¾ cups (4 dl) sprouts.

QUINOA

White quinoa is easy to sprout, and the process goes incredibly fast. The seeds will sprout one-quarter-inch tails in just thirty-six hours. They'll be soft but still have some chew. Unfortunately, red and black quinoa are very challenging to sprout. A few small seeds will produce a tiny tail, but most of them never make it out of the starting blocks. It's the same for quinoa cultivation in South America, where red and black quinoas are also very difficult to produce; this is reflected in their retail price at the grocery store.

Once, it was recommended to rinse quinoa before using it to remove the bitter compound saponin, which is on the exterior of the seed. Nowadays, quinoa is rinsed before it is packaged.

Quinoa is grown and widely consumed in South America. It made its appearance in the West over the last decade and has since become one of the trendiest seeds on the market. What makes quinoa interesting is, first and foremost, its protein content; it also contains good fats and fiber. That it is gluten-free has helped to hype it even more. Quinoa is related to plants like spinach and beets.

SUITABLE FOR

Sprouted quinoa is soft but still retains good chew. It has a slight nutlike flavor with a touch of bitterness. It's very good raw in salads. The sprouts are also good in breads, made into oatmeal, or roasted for granola.

WHERE TO FIND THEM

Make sure to buy white quinoa. Even though the labels say white, the color can vary from white to beige or even to slightly pink. Quinoa is also sold as puffs and flakes, but these cannot be used for sprouting. Red and black quinoa are difficult to sprout, and the same applies for the contents of packs of mixed color quinoa.

METHOD

All discussed methods work. Use a fine-mesh sieve instead of a colander, otherwise the small seeds might fall through the holes.

HOW TO

Choose one of the discussed methods. If the quinoa foams when it's being rinsed, continue rinsing it until the foaming stops. Quinoa sprouts in record time; there are signs of little tails as soon as after half a day. Then the process speeds up even more, so taste the sprouts as you go along. Quinoa sprouts are ready typically after twenty-four to thirty-six hours. If they're left to sprout longer, they risk taking on a sour, slightly yeasty flavor.

Quinoa sprouts especially quickly during the summer, so sprout the quinoa in the refrigerator if it's very warm inside. It will take longer, but you'll have better control over the process and you'll get fresher results.

Soak time: At least 6 hours, but preferably overnight.
Sprouting time after soaking: Approximately 24 to 36 hours
Yield: Quinoa: approx. 2½ oz (70 g) or 3⅓ fl oz (1 dl) will yield approx. 5¼ oz (150 g) or 1¾ cups (4 dl) of sprouts.

SESAME SEEDS

You can sprout both white and black sesame seeds, but sprouted black sesame seeds tend to turn bitter fast. Time is of the essence here, so sprout the seeds quickly over a couple of days; after that they become too bitter. Choose white sesame seeds in their hulls; they're beige with a slightly matte surface. The hulled seeds that are whiter and shiny cannot be used for sprouting.

Use the small, fine-mesh sieve method for sprouting. Soak the seeds for at least an hour, but preferably overnight. Use the sprouts in Asian dressings, in a stir-fry, or as a coating for vegetarian burgers. The sprouts are also good in cookies, added to oatmeal, or blended in a smoothie.

CAN WE SPROUT NUTS?

Walnuts, hazelnuts (filberts), almonds, and all other nuts are also seeds, of course. But can they be sprouted? Weeell . . . Whoever is willing to wait for a sprout from a nut might have a long wait ahead. However, what I recommend for nuts—if they're untreated—is to soak them for a few hours. That way their enzymes are activated just like in other seeds and their nutrients become more available.

These days, specialty shops and online vendors sell "activated nuts," which cost a fortune. These are nuts that have been soaked for eight hours and might have been "sprouted" for a day or two, after which they have been dried in a dehydrator (or in a regular oven at around 104°F/40°C). The nuts need to be thoroughly dry, otherwise they can easily develop mold.

Anyone who makes nut milks is familiar with the process, but in this case, the nuts are just soaked without being dehydrated. After soaking, the nuts are processed in a blender and then strained off, leaving their "milk" behind.

RECIPES
SPROUTS

TUTTI FRUTTI ALFALFA SMOOTHIE

Mild sprouts work well in smoothies. They add wholesomeness without overpowering the drink's flavor. If you don't like banana, you can make the smoothie creamy by adding avocado instead.

MAKES 2 GLASSES

1¾ oz (50 g) or 6¾ fl oz (2 dl) alfalfa or mung
    bean sprouts
6¾ fl oz (2 dl) raspberries
6¾ fl oz (2 dl) orange juice
1 banana, peeled and frozen
1 tbsp honey (optional)

Blend everything until you have a lump-free smoothie, preferably using a countertop blender, although an immersion blender will work, too.

Pour the smoothie into glasses, and why not garnish it with a pinch of sprouted strands?

MANGO SMOOTHIE WITH SPROUTS & ROSEHIPS

A true blast of vitamins that flirts with the flavor of rosehip soup. Remember to blend this smoothie thoroughly since it's most delicious when it's completely smooth.

MAKES 2 GLASSES

1¾ oz (50 g) or 6¾ fl oz (2 dl) alfalfa or mung
    bean sprouts
6¾ fl oz (2 dl) mango, diced and frozen
6¾ fl oz (2 dl) orange juice
6¾ fl oz (2 dl) almond milk
1 tbsp rosehip powder
1 tbsp honey (optional)

Mix all the ingredients until they become a lump-free smoothie, preferably using a countertop blender, although an immersion blender will work, too.

Pour the smoothie into glasses, and top it with some sprouts.

APRICOT AND CHIA TRIFLE

Chia pudding is heightened here with some crispy sprouts, thick yogurt, and apricots. Trifle really is just a layered dessert, but who cares? It sounds more delectable than plain old pudding!

SERVES 2

3½ fl oz (1 dl) coconut milk (or almond or cow's milk)

4 tsp chia seeds

¹⁄₁₀ tsp vanilla powder

10 dried apricots + 6¾ fl oz (2 dl) water

Some liquid honey (optional)

1 apple

3½ fl oz (1 dl) Turkish yogurt (10%)

Approx. 3½ fl oz (1 dl) mixed sprouts (quinoa, buckwheat, and sunflower sprouts, for example)

Hemp hearts, coconut chips, and nuts, for garnish

Mix the coconut milk, chia seeds, and vanilla powder in a bowl. Let sit in the refrigerator for at least 2 hours, but preferably overnight.

Bring water to a boil in a small saucepan. Remove from the heat, add the apricots, put a lid on the pan, and let the apricots steep for about 30 minutes or until they are soft. Drain the water from the apricots, saving the water. Mix the apricots with an immersion blender, adding back some of the reserved water until the texture is thick and smooth. Sweeten with some honey, if desired.

Cut the apple into small dice.

Layer the chia pudding, yogurt, apricot purée, and sprouts in 2 glasses. Garnish with diced apple, hemp hearts, coconut chips, and nuts.

SPROUTED SEED BREAD

A bread loaded with energy and other good stuff. It's best to wrap the finished loaf in a kitchen towel and let it rest for a few hours before cutting into it. This gives it time to settle properly and hold together better. It's perfect for slicing and storing in the freezer, so you can toast some as needed.

MAKES 1 LOAF

Oil, for the baking pan
1 tbsp psyllium husk
3⅓ fl oz (1 dl) flaxseeds
3⅓ fl oz (1 dl) sesame seeds
6¾ fl oz (2 dl) boiling water
6¾ fl oz (2 dl) oat flour
7 oz (200 g) sprouted
  buckwheat
1 tsp baking soda
1½ tsp salt
5 fl oz (1½ dl) yogurt (3%)
3⅓ fl oz (1 dl) dark Swedish
  beet syrup*
3⅓ fl oz (1 dl) roasted pumpkin
  or sunflower seeds
3⅓ fl oz (1 dl) roasted
  hazelnuts (filberts)
Oat flour, for dusting

Preheat the oven to 390°F (200°C). Oil a 2-quart (2 liter) bread pan.

Mix the psyllium husk, flaxseeds, and sesame seeds together in a large bowl. Pour in the boiling water and mix thoroughly. Let the mix rise for 10 minutes.

Add the oat flour, sprouted buckwheat, baking soda, salt, yogurt, and syrup to the seed mixture. Mix well with an electric handheld mixer for a few minutes until everything is thoroughly combined.

Stir in the pumpkin seeds and nuts.

Pour the batter into the bread pan and sprinkle with some oat flour. Cover and let it rest for about 30 minutes.

Bake in the lower half of the oven for about 1 hour. Let the bread sit for at least half an hour before removing it from the pan.

Tip!

If you have enough sprouts and two loaf pans, make two loaves. It's always convenient to have some extra bread in the freezer.

*Swedish beet syrup can't be replaced with corn syrup because of the difference in flavor. The beet syrup can be found online.

SPICY QUINOA CRACKERS

Crispy seed crackers with a taste of fennel. It's a little awkward to turn the cracker when it comes time to bake it on the other side; fortunately, it doesn't matter if it breaks because it's meant to be broken into pieces later anyway.

MAKES 1 BAKING SHEET
1 tsp fennel seeds
3½ oz (100 g) sprouted quinoa
3⅓ fl oz (1 dl) flaxseeds
6¾ fl oz (2 dl) pumpkin seeds
1¾ fl oz (½ dl) sesame seeds
2 tsp psyllium husk
1 tsp herb salt
5 fl oz (1½ dl) water
1 tbsp honey
1 tbsp canola oil
⅕ tsp salt flakes

Tip!

Store the crackers in a dry place. If they still soften a bit, dry them out in the oven for 20 minutes at 210°F (100°C) or run them in the microwave for a few seconds.

Preheat oven to 350°F (175°C).

Crush the fennel seeds lightly with a mortar and pestle.

Mix the quinoa sprouts, flaxseeds, pumpkin seeds, sesame seeds, psyllium husk, herb salt, and crushed fennel seeds in a bowl.

Bring the water to a boil, and add the honey and oil. Stir the hot liquid into the seed mixture and mix thoroughly.

On the kitchen counter, place the dough between two sheets of parchment paper. With a rolling pin, roll out the dough thinly between the parchment paper. Place the paper on a baking sheet. Remove the top sheet of paper. Sprinkle the dough with some salt flakes and push them into the dough lightly with your hand.

Bake on the middle rack of the oven for about 20 minutes. Remove the paper with the dough. Carefully turn the dough over onto the baking sheet so the flip side can cook. Carefully pull off the other sheet of parchment paper. Bake for another 10 minutes, and keep a close eye on things so the cracker doesn't burn.

Let the cracker cool on a cooling rack, and then break it into pieces. Store the crackers in a dry and airtight container. The crackers pair well with cheese and a few sprouts or with some yellow hummus (see the recipe on p. 70).

SPROUTED GRANOLA

Sprouted buckwheat develops a fine flavor and a delicious crunch when it's roasted in the oven. Granola is a great way to clean out the pantry. Use the seeds, nuts, and dried fruit that you have in your kitchen at the moment.

MAKES ABOUT 2 QUARTS (2 LITERS)

A generous 1 lb. (500 g) sprouted buckwheat

3⅓ fl oz (1 dl) flaxseeds

1 tbsp ground cinnamon

2 tbsp rosehip powder

⅖ tsp salt

1¼ cups (3 dl) nuts and seeds (hazelnuts (filberts), almonds, sunflower seeds, pumpkin seeds, for example)

3⅓ fl oz (1 dl) canola oil

5 fl oz (1½ dl) liquid honey

3⅓ fl oz (1 dl) coconut chips

5 fl oz (1½ dl) dried fruit (apricots, raisins, dried redcurrants, blueberries, or Goji berries, for example)

Preheat the oven to 350°F (175°C).

Mix the sprouted buckwheat, flaxseeds, cinnamon, rosehip powder, salt, nuts, and seeds in a large bowl.

Mix the oil and honey. Pour this mixture over the seed mixture. Mix everything well with your hands.

Transfer this mixture to a rimmed baking sheet lined with parchment paper. Roast it on the lower rack of the oven for 20 to 30 minutes. Stir the mixture midway through. Keep a close watch toward the end so the mixture doesn't burn.

Take the baking sheet out of the oven and let the mixture cool. Mix in coconut chips and dried fruit.

Store the granola in a jar with a tight-fitting lid.

Quinoa granola!

Use an identical amount of sprouted quinoa instead of buckwheat. Or use half of each.

SPROUTED BUCKWHEAT AND POPPY SEED PANCAKES

Classic French—Breton—galettes are made with buckwheat flour. Here we make fluffy pancakes from sprouted buckwheat. The poppy seeds add crunch. We serve the pancakes with delicious blueberry mascarpone frosting. Serve as a sumptuous breakfast or brunch.

MAKES APPROX. 25 PANCAKES

5¼ oz (150 g) sprouted buckwheat

6¾ fl oz cow's milk (or almond or oat milk)

2 large eggs

½ tsp baking powder

⅕ tsp vanilla powder

⅕ tsp salt

1 tbsp poppy seeds

1 tbsp butter

Confectioner's sugar, for dusting (optional)

With an immersion blender, mix the sprouted buckwheat, milk, eggs, baking powder, vanilla powder, salt, and poppy seeds to make a smooth batter.

Melt the butter, then add it to the batter.

Fry the pancakes in butter on a griddle (or make crepes in a regular frying pan). Serve with mascarpone topping (see below) and sprinkle everything with confectioner's sugar, if desired.

Mascarpone frosting with blueberries

In a bowl, mix 3⅓ fl oz (1 dl) mascarpone cheese, 3⅓ fl oz (1 dl) Turkish yogurt (10%), 1 tbsp honey, and the grated rind of half a lemon. Add 3⅓ fl oz (1 dl) frozen blueberries. Let the mix sit for about 5 minutes, and then carefully stir it with a spoon.

SPICY CURRIED LENTIL SOUP

This soup can be made with green lentil sprouts, but the red lentil sprouts provide a more beautiful color. Season it with sambal oelek and sample it as you go along, always starting with small amounts.

SERVES 4

1 onion
1 clove garlic
1 carrot
2 tbsp canola oil
½ tbsp curry powder
10½ oz (300 g) red lentil sprouts
1 tsp ground ginger
1 stick cinnamon
1 vegetable stock cube
½ tsp salt
2 cups (5 dl) water
1 can of coconut milk (13½ fl oz/400 ml)
1½ tbsp freshly squeezed lemon juice
½ tsp sambal oelek
Turkish yogurt, shoots, and maybe some chili powder and/or paprika, for serving

Peel and chop the onion and garlic. Peel and slice the carrot. In a saucepan, sauté the onion and garlic in oil over medium heat for about 5 minutes, taking care not to brown them. Add in the curry powder at the last minute.

Add in the carrot, lentil sprouts, ginger, cinnamon, stock cube, salt, water, and coconut milk. Cover the saucepan and simmer everything for about 15 to 20 minutes, or until the lentils and carrot have softened.

Remove the cinnamon stick, then purée the soup until smooth with an immersion blender. Add the lemon juice and sambal oelek. If needed, add some more lemon juice, sambal oelek, and salt, to taste.

Enjoy the soup with a dollop of Turkish yogurt and some extra shoots, such as broccoli or cress shoots.

BEET AND LENTIL BURGERS WITH FETA CHEESE

These are really good veggie burgers! It's important to let the mix sit for fifteen minutes so the oats have a chance to swell and soften and the burgers hold their shape in the skillet.

SERVES 4

7 oz (200 g) beets
1 garlic clove
7 oz (200 g) sprouted lentils or quinoa
6¾ fl oz (2 dl) rolled oats
1 egg
1 tbsp chopped basil
²/₅ tsp salt
¹/₅ tsp black pepper
5¼ oz (150 g) feta cheese
2 tbsp pine nuts
Canola oil
Wheat buns, sprouts, shoots, and avocado mayo (see recipe on p. 122), for serving

Peel and grate the beets finely with a box grater. Peel and crush the garlic.

Coarsely chop the lentil sprouts in a food processor or with an immersion blender. If you're using quinoa sprouts, you don't need to chop them.

Add the grated beets, garlic, oats, egg, basil, salt, and black pepper to the mixed lentil (or quinoa) sprouts.

Transfer the mixture to a bowl. Add in crumbled feta cheese and pine nuts and mix gently. Let the mixture sit for at least 15 minutes.

Shape into four burger patties (this is easier to do if you oil your hands first).

Cook the burgers in plenty of oil in a large skillet, about 4 minutes per side, or until they are nicely browned.

Toast or heat the buns, and serve with the accompaniments.

PAD THAI WITH TOFU & ADZUKI SPROUTS

A classic pad thai is made with mung bean sprouts, but why not try making it with some snazzy adzuki sprouts instead? They add a bit more satisfying chew to the dish.

SERVES 4

1 (9½ oz [270 g]) pack of tofu

2 tbsp fish sauce

2 tbsp freshly squeezed lime juice

2 tbsp brown sugar

1 (8¾ oz [250 g]) pack of rice noodles

Canola oil

2 garlic cloves

1 fresh red chili

2 carrots

4 scallions

14 oz (400 g) adzuki (or mung bean) sprouts

2 large eggs

3⅓ fl oz (1 dl) salted peanuts and cilantro, coarsely chopped, for garnish

Lime wedges, for serving (optional)

Start by marinating the tofu. Cut the tofu into approximately ¼-inch (1 cm) dice and put them in a bowl. Mix the fish sauce, lime, and sugar in another bowl. Save half the sauce, and mix the rest in with the tofu. Let marinate while proceeding with the rest of the recipe.

Prepare the noodles according to the instructions on the package. Drain, rinse them in cold water, and drain them again. Mix the noodles with 1 tablespoon of canola oil, and set them aside.

In a large skillet, sauté the tofu (along with the marinade) in oil over medium heat for about 2 minutes. Remove the tofu from the skillet and set it aside.

Peel and finely chop the garlic. Halve, seed, and julienne the red chili. Peel and cut the carrots into matchsticks. Julienne the scallions.

Over high heat and using plenty of oil in the large skillet, sauté the garlic, chili, and carrot sticks for about 2 minutes, stirring often to prevent burning. Add the sprouts and half the scallions, and sauté for another minute.

Lower the heat to medium high. Push the vegetables to one side of the skillet. Add in the eggs one at a time. Keep stirring while cooking them so they look like scrambled eggs.

Once the eggs have cooked, add the tofu and noodles. Let everything cook and heat through. Add the remaining sauce.

Sprinkle with peanuts, the remaining scallions, and cilantro. Serve with lime wedges, if desired.

SUSHI ROLLS WITH QUINOA AND WASABI MAYO

Make fresh sushi with sprouted quinoa instead of rice.

SERVES 4

1½ tbsp rice vinegar
1½ tbsp sugar
½ tsp salt
10½ oz (300 g) or approx.
    2½ cups (6 dl) sprouted white
    quinoa
½ English (hothouse) cucumber
2 avocados
Approx. 2 tbsp Gari (sweet
    pickled ginger)
8 nori sheets
Mixed shoots—pea, mustard,
    radish, or cress, for example

Wasabi mayo

Mix 6¾ fl oz (2 dl) mayonnaise with 1–2 teaspoons of wasabi powder and 1 teaspoon of Japanese soy sauce.

Mix the rice vinegar, sugar, and salt, and let sit for about 5 minutes or until the sugar has dissolved. Add in the quinoa sprouts.

Cut the cucumber in half length wise, and cut the halves into approximately 6 inch (15 cm)–long sticks, slightly less than ¼-inch (½ cm) thick. Halve the avocados and remove the pits. Scoop out the avocado flesh with a large tablespoon and slice it lengthwise. Cut the Gari into smaller chunks.

Place a thin kitchen towel or a bamboo mat on the kitchen counter. Put a nori sheet in the middle, glossy side down.

Spread the quinoa sprouts evenly over the nori sheet, but leave ½ to ¾ inch (1–2 cm) empty along the upper edge of the sheet so you can close the sushi roll.

Place the cucumber sticks, avocado, Gari, and maybe a few shoots in a line about ¾ inch (2 cm) in from the edge nearest to you.

Carefully, but as tightly as you can, roll up the nori sheet. Make sure the filling doesn't get pushed out forward. Roll the sheet until you've almost reached the upper edge. Press the roll together and hold it like this for a little while. Moisten the upper edge of the nori sheet with some water and finishing rolling the sushi together. Repeat with the rest of the nori sheets.

Cut the rolls into approximately ¾ inch (2 cm)–thick slices, and transfer them to a platter. Add a dollop of wasabi mayo on each slice, and serve the remaining mayo with the sushi. Garnish with shoots. Serve this dish with Japanese soy sauce preferably, or with soy dip with mustard and sesame (see p. 73).

WINTER SALAD WITH BUCKWHEAT AND HALLOUMI CHEESE

A sprouted version of an old standby from many years back, it works as a green pick-me-up dish amid the Christmas fare, as well as a colorful lunch salad.

SERVES 4

10½ oz (300 g) Brussels sprouts
Olive oil, for frying
Salt
Black pepper
14 oz (400 g) sprouted buckwheat
1 orange
4 dried figs
½ pomegranate
2 tbsp chopped parsley
2 tbsp olive oil
½ tsp salt flakes
⅕ tsp ground black pepper
1¾ fl oz (½ dl), walnuts, preferably toasted (optional)
7 oz (200 g) halloumi cheese

Clean and cut the Brussels sprouts in half. In a large skillet, sauté them in plenty of oil for about 5 minutes. Season with salt and pepper. Add in the buckwheat. Sauté about 2 minutes, stirring constantly. Let the mixture cool down a little.

Peel the orange with a knife; cut out wedges of orange without any pith. Julienne the figs. Remove the seeds from the pomegranate and remove the white membranes. The easiest way to do this is to hold the pomegranate cut-side down over a bowl and loosen the seeds so they fall into the bowl.

Mix the Brussels sprouts with the parsley, oil, and salt flakes, and season with salt and pepper to taste. Layer with orange wedges and figs on a platter or in a bowl, and sprinkle with pomegranate seeds and walnuts.

Slice the halloumi and fry it in a skillet over high heat, about 1 minute per side. Top the salad with the halloumi slices.

SNAZZY FALAFEL

I never deep-fry falafel. It's enough to just fry it in plenty of oil to achieve the right level of crispiness. Depending on how sprouted your peas are, you might need to use more or less cornstarch. You'll have to test it, starting with small amounts.

SERVES 4
1 yellow onion
1 garlic clove
14 oz (400 g) sprouted yellow peas
3⅓ fl oz (1 dl) parsley, finely
   chopped
1 tsp cumin
1 tsp dried coriander
½ tbsp baking powder
1¾–3⅓ fl oz (½–1 dl) cornstarch
1 tsp sambal oelek
1 tsp salt
Olive oil, for frying

Peel, halve, and finely chop the onion and garlic. Put all ingredients except oil in a food processor and blend till you have a smooth mixture. Add more cornstarch if the mixture seems too wet. If it looks dry, you can add in extra tablespoons of water.

Turn this mixture into 16 puck-shaped patties.

In a skillet, fry the patties in plenty of oil, about 3 minutes per side. Drain them on paper towels. Stuff them into pita bread or tortillas, and enjoy them accompanied by sunflower shoots or lettuce, maybe some sprouted hummus (see p. 70), and quick-preserved red onion (see below).

Quick-preserved red onion

Peel, halve, and thinly slice a red onion. Place it in a small bowl and add 1 tablespoon of white or red wine vinegar and ⅕ teaspoon salt. Mix well and let sit for at least 20 minutes, stirring the onion now and then.

NOODLE SOUP WITH COCONUT, SPROUTS & SHOOTS

My colleague Sofia is a true pro when it comes to developing recipes. This soup is a favorite in our home. Simple to make, it's warming thanks to just the right amount of bite from the chili.

SERVES 4

1 (8¾ oz [250 g]) pack of noodles
1 tbsp canola oil
1 carrot
2 tsp red curry paste
Canola oil, for frying
1 (13½ fl oz [400 ml]) can of coconut milk
1 tsp tomato purée
2 tbsp fish sauce (or Japanese soy sauce)
1 vegetable stock cube
1 tsp sugar
1¼ cups (3 dl) water
2 tsp freshly squeezed lime juice
1 red bell pepper
About 7 oz (200 g) mung bean sprouts
Pea and radish shoots, for garnish

Prepare the noodles according to the instructions on the package. Drain off the water and mix the noodles with the oil.

Peel and thinly slice the carrot.

In a saucepan, cook the curry paste and carrot in some oil for about 1 minute.

Add in the coconut milk, tomato purée, fish sauce, stock cube, sugar, and water, and cook about 5 minutes. Add in the lime juice.

Halve, seed, and julienne the bell pepper; add it to the soup.

Divide the noodles between the bowls, add the soup, and sprinkle with sprouts and shoots.

STIR-FRIED MUNG BEANS WITH FRENCH-STYLE GREEN BEANS & ROASTED ONIONS

You can't be stingy with the oil here. You'll need plenty of oil in the skillet to achieve the right crispiness. Sauté the food, stirring it so it doesn't burn.

SERVES 4
¾-inch (2 cm) piece of fresh ginger
3 garlic cloves
3 tbsp canola oil
⅕ tsp chili flakes
7 oz (200 g) fresh or frozen green beans (haricots verts)
10½ oz (300 g) sprouted mung beans
1 tbsp Japanese soy sauce
2 tsp sugar
⅕ tsp salt
2 tbsp roasted onions (canned)

Peel and chop the ginger and garlic.

Heat the oil in a skillet. Fry the garlic, ginger, and chili flakes over high heat for about 2 minutes, stirring constantly. Don't let things brown too much.

Stir in the green beans and mung bean sprouts.

Add the soy sauce, sugar, and salt. Sauté for about 5 minutes, or until all the liquid has evaporated, stirring constantly.

Sprinkle with roasted onions before serving.

KOREAN CUCUMBER SALAD WITH SPROUTS

The texture of mung bean sprouts changes completely when they're cooked. Their crispness disappears and they take on an almost meaty, solid quality. They go well with most dishes featuring noodles and rice, like bibimpap and fried rice for instance, but also with sautéed fish and grilled meats.

MAKES 3½ CUPS (8 DL)
10½ oz (300 g) mung bean sprouts
1 English (hothouse) cucumber
1 garlic clove
1 tsp Sriracha sauce (or 1 tsp chili flakes)
1½ tbsp sesame oil
1½ tbsp fish sauce (or Japanese soy sauce)
1 tbsp rice vinegar
1 tbsp toasted sesame seeds

In a large saucepan, bring lightly salted water to a boil. Add in the mung bean sprouts and bring back to a boil, then immediately transfer the sprouts to a colander. Rinse the sprouts in cold water and let them drain.

With a mandolin or cheese slicer, slice the cucumber at a slant. Put the cucumber slices in a colander and, using your hands, press out their liquid.

Peel and finely chop the garlic.

Mix together the garlic, Sriracha sauce, sesame oil, fish sauce, and vinegar.

Mix the sprouts and cucumber slices with the sauce; sprinkle with sesame seeds. Let the salad sit for about half an hour, preferably, to let the flavors blend.

TAHINI DRESSING

Tahini is one of those things that occasionally takes a while for people to understand what the fuss is all about. After all, the flavor is mostly bitter—and fatty. But as you continue to use sesame paste, it can easily become addictive. These days, I'm hooked!

APPROX. 5 FL OZ (1½ DL)
1¾ fl oz (½ dl) tahini
1 tbsp Japanese soy sauce
½ tsp honey
1 tsp freshly squeezed lime juice
½ crushed garlic clove
1¾ fl oz (½ dl) water
1 tbsp sprouted sesame seeds

Mix the tahini, soy sauce, honey, lime juice, and garlic in a bowl.

Continue mixing while adding water in a thin, even stream. Dilute with more water if the dressing is too thick.

Stir in the sprouted sesame seeds.

SPROUTED HUMMUS

"Make hummus, not war!" Every Middle Eastern family has their own recipe for hummus. Naturally, there has to be a sprouted version of it, too. With a jar of hummus in the refrigerator, I can always cobble together some kind of dish for lunch or dinner.

APPROX. 6¾ FL OZ (2 DL)
7 oz (200 g) sprouted chickpeas (or yellow peas)
1 garlic clove
2 tbsp tahini
2 tbsp freshly squeezed lemon juice
½ tsp sambal oelek
⅕ tsp cumin
½ tsp salt
4 tbsp olive oil

Put the sprouted peas in a small saucepan, and cover them with water. Bring the water to a boil and cook the peas for 10 minutes. Pour off the water.

Peel and finely chop the garlic.

Mix the peas in a food processor or with an immersion blender, along with the garlic, tahini, lemon juice, sambal oelek, cumin, salt, and oil.

Dilute with some water if the hummus seems too thick.

Yellow hummus

Turmeric adds nice color to hummus. But sample the hummus as you add it in—some enjoy the taste of turmeric, others less so. Start with ½ teaspoon per recipe.

SOY DIP WITH SESAME SEED SPROUTS & MUSTARD SHOOTS

It's bit surprising to encounter Dijon mustard in an Asian sauce, but give it a shot: the flavors work well together. The mustard also helps bind the dressing to give it that creamy consistency. You can try the dip with salmon, among other things; it is very versatile.

APPROX. 5 FL OZ (1½ DL)
1¾ fl oz (½ dl) Japanese soy
   sauce
½ tbsp honey
1 tbsp Dijon mustard
1½ tbsp olive oil
1 tbsp sesame oil
1 tbsp rice or white wine vinegar
1 tbsp sprouted sesame seeds
2 tbsp mustard shoots

Whisk together the soy sauce, honey, mustard, olive oil, sesame oil, and vinegar to make a smooth dip.

Add in the sesame seeds, and sprinkle with some snipped mustard shoots.

BAKED SQUASH WITH LENTIL SPROUTS & ALMOND PESTO

Lentil sprouts add a nice crunch to the soft, sweet winter squash. If you can't find squash, use sweet potatoes instead.

SERVES 4

2¼ lb (1 kg) squash (butternut, for
  example)
3 tbsp olive oil
1 tsp salt
1 recipe almond pesto with
  arugula & lemon (see p. 124)
7 oz (200 g) black lentil sprouts
Arugula shoots, for sprinkling
  (optional)

Preheat the oven to 435°F (225°C).

Peel and cut the squash into approximately 1-inch (3 cm) cubes, and place them on a baking sheet lined with parchment paper. Mix with oil and salt.

Bake the squash on the middle rack of the oven for about 20 minutes or until soft.

Mix half the pesto with the lentil sprouts.

Sprinkle the sprouts over the squash. Add on dollops of the remaining pesto and, if desired, sprinkle with arugula shoots.

CRISP WASABI PEAS

A fun version of the wasabi nut snack. Green pea sprouts add pretty color, and it's just as delicious with sprouted chickpeas or yellow peas.

SERVES 2

7 oz (200 g) sprouted green
  peas
2 tbsp cornstarch
Canola oil
1–2 tsp wasabi powder
1 tsp salt flakes

Transfer the sprouted peas onto a paper towel. Dry them as much and as carefully as you can.

Place the peas in a bowl and carefully turn to coat them with the cornstarch.

Heat plenty of canola oil in a high-sided frying pan. Fry the peas over high heat for about 2 minutes, stirring occasionally. Sprinkle in the wasabi powder and salt flakes, stir some more, and cook for another 1 minute or until the peas are golden and crunchy.

Transfer the cooked peas to a paper towel to drain. Serve the peas immediately, because the peas lose their crunch quite quickly.

Or curried peas!

Substitute ½ teaspoon curry powder and ⅕ teaspoon chili pepper for the wasabi powder, then follow the recipe for the wasabi peas.

QUINOA AND PEANUT BARS

These are versatile bars—enjoy them as an energy booster before or after exercise or as a treat with a cup of coffee. The sprouts add a tasty crunch.

MAKES 20 SMALL BARS
8 fresh dates
3½ fl oz (1 dl) walnuts
4½ oz (125 g) sprouted quinoa
  (or buckwheat)
5 fl oz (1½ dl) peanut butter
1¾ fl oz (½ dl) coconut
3 tbsp flaxseeds
2 tbsp liquid honey
1 large egg
⅕ tsp salt

Preheat the oven to 255°F (125°C). Remove the dates' stones, and finely chop the dates. Chop the walnuts.

Place all the ingredients in a large bowl and mix thoroughly to make a smooth paste.

Press the mixture into a jelly roll pan lined with parchment paper, about 9¾ x 6 inches (25 x 15 cm). The paste will stick less if you wet your hands slightly before handling it.

Place the pan on the middle rack of the oven and bake for about 45 minutes. Remove the pan from the oven and let it cool a little.

Transfer the parchment paper to a cutting board. Cut into 20 bars.

Wrap the bars individually in plastic wrap or parchment paper to make them easy to take along. Store them in the refrigerator or freezer.

COFFEE AND COCONUT TRUFFLES WITH ROASTED BUCKWHEAT

These truffles are especially delicious if you roast both the sprouted buckwheat and the coconut.

MAKES ABOUT 20 TRUFFLES
2¾ oz (75 g) sprouted buckwheat
10 fl oz (3 dl) grated coconut
12 fresh dates
3⅓ fl oz (1 dl) nuts (pecans, cashews, or hazelnuts/filberts, for example)
½ tsp vanilla powder
3 tbsp cold espresso coffee
²/₅ tsp salt flakes
2 tbsp cocoa
Grated coconut, cocoa, macha powder, chopped nuts, or sesame seeds, to coat

Roast the sprouted buckwheat and the coconut in a dry skillet for 3 to 4 minutes while stirring constantly. Keep a close eye on the skillet and remove it from the heat once the coconut develops some color and the sprouts are dry. Let them cool a little.

Remove the stones from the dates.

Place all the ingredients in a food processor and mix them to make a paste.

Form balls with the paste, and roll them in coconut, cocoa, macha powder, chopped nuts, or seeds.

Store the truffles in the refrigerator or freezer.

TAMARI-ROASTED SUNFLOWER SPROUTS

Roast sunflower sprouts in a skillet to make a crunchy snack. Use chili powder instead of herbs if you like things spicy.

5¼ oz (150 g) (approx. 1¼ cups [3 dl]) sunflower
   sprouts
1 tbsp tamari (or other Japanese soy sauce)
Optional: Grated peel of ½ a lemon and
   1 tsp fresh herbs (thyme and rosemary, for
   example)

Place the sprouts in a dry, warm skillet. Add in the tamari and mix. Cook on medium heat while stirring until all the liquid has evaporated.

Continue to roast the sprouts, stirring now and then and keeping a close eye on things so the sprouts don't burn. Cook the sprouts until they're golden and completely dry (they will crackle a bit).

Add chopped or freshly picked herbs and grated lemon peel, if desired. Transfer to a plate and let cool.

SPROUTED SUNFLOWER BARK

Honey and sprouts become a crunchy bark. Enjoy it as is or break it over a salad. It also makes a delicious topping for ice cream.

5¼ oz (150 g) (approx. 1¼ cups [3 dl]) sunflower
   sprouts
1¾ fl oz (½ dl) honey
⅕ tsp salt flakes

Place the sunflower sprouts in a dry, hot skillet. Fry them while stirring until all the liquid has evaporated.

Lower the heat and cook the sprouts until they're completely dry (they will crackle and snap a bit). Continue to stir, keeping a close eye on them so they don't burn.

Pour in the honey, stir, and let it boil for 1 minute.

Pour the bark immediately onto a sheet of parchment paper. Spread out the mixture and sprinkle with salt flakes. Let it cool, and break into pieces.

SHOOTS & MICROGREENS

Spread a handful of seeds over some paper, soil, or on a mesh grid over water and you will be able to harvest delicate shoots after a week. And you can do this year-round. Microgreens is just another term for shoots, but it's a very good name because we're dealing with micro-size greens, after all. You can use the shoots to mix up an arugula pesto, round out a broccoli salad, or jazz up some spring rolls.

Microgreens, or shoots, are merely plants harvested very early. Microgreens differ from sprouts in that you cut off and eat only the stalk and leaves, but not the seeds and roots. Most microgreens are ready to be eaten after one to two weeks; that's when they've developed the first two small leaves, also called cotyledon. These look pretty similar across most plants, and it's early in the next stage when the true leaves appear that plants take on their characteristic appearance.

Unlike sprouts, which develop in the dark, shoots distinguish themselves by using the energy they take in from sunlight and converting it to green chlorophyll. However, they must first go through the same stage as sprouts.

Many of the seeds we eat can be cultivated into shoots, provided they haven't been treated in some way that impedes their capacity to grow. However, not all shoots are tasty. Flaxseeds can be found in every grocery store and they grow with nary a protest into fine green shoots. Unfortunately, they also have a very unpleasant, bitter taste. Other shoots quickly become woody and unappetizing. Wheatgrass, for instance, is a shoot considered by the living food community as vital to good health. But like other grasses, it's difficult to eat if you're a human being and not a cow. The solution, therefore, is to extract its juice.

For this chapter, I have chosen shoots that I enjoy eating and that I feel are easy to grow successfully. You'll have to order some of them online, but garden nurseries and even some well-stocked grocery stores will sell seeds for microgreen cultivation.

Soaking

Soaking is best for larger seeds like yellow and green peas, mung beans, and sunflower seeds that are still in their shells. Eight to twelve hours is usually enough, but it's better if they can soak for up to twenty-four hours, which ensures that all the seeds will sprout. Rinse them thoroughly in a colander and put them in plenty of cold water. They swell a lot, so figure three times as much water as seed volume. Make it a habit to go through the seeds after soaking and remove any seeds that have not changed in appearance. Also, remove any damaged or discolored seeds.

Smaller seeds such as broccoli, mustard, and radish can also be soaked, but I usually skip this step here because they start well without it. There is also a category of seeds like arugula, cress, and chia that are not at all suited to soaking: they develop a protective gel-like layer around the seed when they come in contact with water. If you try to soak these seeds, you'll likely end up with a difficult-to-handle, jellied lump. These seeds are easier to grow directly on paper.

Growing

Shoots can be cultivated in many different ways, such as in soil, on paper, or in water (also called hydroponic cultivation).

Growing shoots in soil has its advantages and disadvantages. The plus side is that from the time the seeds have taken hold and germinated, and the shoots have begun to grow, they need very little care. Soil retains moisture much longer than, say, wet paper. One of the drawbacks to growing in soil is, of course, that there is more work at the onset. You risk smudging dirt when you're cutting off the shoots. This is mostly a problem with tiny seeds that don't grow very tall, so it's less complicated to grow them on paper. As for larger shoots, such as sunflower and peas, soil is less of an issue since their stem is much taller.

The general rule for growing shoots is that they should be sown very close together. Shoots don't grow into large plants and so do not develop roots, a sturdy stalk, or full-blown leaves. Thus, they do not require the same amount of space as maturing plants.

<< One-week-old mustard ready for harvest.

Time of year, indoor temperature, light, and heat all affect how quickly and how well shoots grow. But it's surprising how little light shoots need to convert it, and carbon dioxide, to potent energy in the form of green chlorophyll. So don't feel discouraged if you only have a north-facing window and suddenly fancy some radish or arugula shoots in the middle of darkest December; within a week, you'll be ready to harvest some green shoots. Shoots require less light to survive than the same plant when fully grown. However, shoots that take a bit longer—pea and sunflower shoots, for example—will do better if they're exposed to plenty of light while they're growing. If they're situated in too much shade, the shoots will devote most of their energy to reaching toward the light. The shoots then become tall and spindly and have smaller leaves.

Methods

Some shoots will grow happily no matter what, while other shoots have preferred methods. Below each shoot I'll share with you my take on which system works best.

Soil

There's no need for a deep layer of soil to grow shoots; a depth of approximately ¾ to 1¼ inches (2½–3 cm) is plenty. That's why you don't have to grow shoots in flowerpots. However, it is smart to grow them in rimmed flowerpot saucers; use regular potting soil.

An extra safeguard against overwatering is to grow the shoots in perforated trays, which lets excess water run off. A simple tip is to use the plastic trays that grocery stores package their fruit in. Or set up disposable aluminum baking pans; just make some holes at the bottom with a fork. A multilevel sprouting tower works well, too, but use only one level and the collection tray underneath. You can't grow shoots in several layers, because when you

water the shoots, the soil may fall onto the next level and dirty the shoots growing there.

That said, in my experience, growing shoots in containers without drainage works fine; you'll just have to take care not to overwater. Keep the soil damp but not soaked. When growing sunflower shoots—shoots that I think are the most challenging to grow—it's a good idea to use a container with proper drainage.

A super convenient way to cultivate shoots is in a regular milk carton: cut it in half lengthwise. Naturally, it must be thoroughly washed out before being used.

How to: Fill your chosen container with ¾–1⅕ inches (2½–3 cm) of planting soil. Spread the soil out evenly. Water the soil lightly with a plant mister. Spread the seeds (dry or pre-soaked, depending on the seed) evenly over the soil's surface. If you lay down too many seeds in one spot, push them apart with your hand. How closely you sow them will depend on the seed. Larger seeds such as peas, mung beans, and sunflower seeds are sown somewhat more apart. Remember that they swell more as they germinate and the shoots start growing. Small seeds are sown very close together but not on top of one another.

Press down lightly with your hand. The seeds should be anchored in the soil (but not covered in soil or pushed into the soil). Wet the seeds once more with the mister, and make sure all seeds are damp.

The container can be out on the kitchen counter, but aim for a darker spot rather than direct sunlight. At this early stage, the seeds have no use at all for the sun's energy. Even if in their natural environment, the seeds would be in the soil, and I've found that they don't require total darkness to develop well.

Mist the seeds once or twice a day. Test the soil now and then, because if the air is very dry and warm, they may need an extra misting. If you're worried the seeds are going to dry out, or if you know you won't be able to mist them on time, cover the container loosely with plastic wrap—but not airtight (or punch a few small holes in the plastic).

Make a habit of checking the soil to make sure it isn't too wet. The seeds don't need a lot of water at this point.

After one to three days, depending on the seeds, small sprouts emerge. This is when you place the future shoots in the light, preferably on a windowsill. If that's not possible, put them near a window. If you have plastic wrap over the container, you can remove it now. Sometimes I leave it on for a day or two, especially in winter, because the wrap not only retains moisture but also a small amount of warmth generated by the growing shoots. However, in summer, it's important to make sure that things don't get too warm and too damp; it's not supposed to be a sauna in there. The shoots can die of heatstroke.

Continue to mist the burgeoning shoots and make sure the soil is kept moist but not wet. Pinch off tiny pieces to taste-test so you can determine when the shoots taste best. Small seeds will have shoots ready to eat after about five to seven days; larger seeds may need up to ten days and sometimes two weeks before they're good to go.

The spent soil can be reused in garden beds or in compost. Reusing the soil to grow more shoots is a bit chancy, as there will be seed leftovers in the soil that might rot when the soil is dampened anew for the next batch of seeds.

Paper

Growing seeds on paper is very neat. Many of you may have childhood memories of scattering cress seeds over damp paper towels or a strip of cotton, and then witnessing the small seeds spring to life. Paper cultivation is suitable, primarily, for small and quick-growing shoots like arugula, radish, cress, and broccoli. The cress method still works, but forget the messy cotton—who wants to eat fuzzy shoots?

Besides, it's difficult to spread seeds evenly over cotton, and it's also an unnecessary cost when you can do just as well with regular kitchen paper towels.

You can buy special "seed paper" (often geared to a specific product, like a sprouting tower with the different levels in the shape of circles). It is easy to use, of course, but I still stick by the humble paper towel.

The paper method isn't all that different from growing seeds in soil—except it's a bit simpler. Here, too, you can use either a container with drainage to allow excess water to drain off or a container without drainage. A simple plate or a flowerpot saucer is fine. Thoroughly washed milk cartons cut in half lengthwise work here as well.

If you own a multilevel sprout tower, the paper method is ideal. You'll be able to grow a few different types of seeds simultaneously on a small surface. Place seed paper or paper towels on each level.

How to: Select a container or plate, and place a sheet of seed paper or a paper towel folded up three or four times onto it. Spray the paper with a flower mister until it is completely soaked and is lying flat. If the paper buckles or becomes lopsided, it will be difficult to spread out the seeds evenly. Spread the seeds (presoaked or dry, depending on the seed) evenly over the paper. Put them close together, but not so close that the seeds end up piled on top of each other. Mist the seeds and make sure they are all damp.

Since paper dries out much faster than soil, I usually cover the container with a piece of plastic wrap, leaving a gap so the container isn't airtight (as an alternative, poke a few small holes in the plastic). If you're using a sprouting tower, the simplest thing to do is put a clean plastic bag over the entire thing to maintain moisture.

You can keep the seed container on the kitchen counter, but in a spot with some shadow rather than in direct sunlight. Cover the seeds with a towel if the light is too intense; seeds can't use the sun's

CULTIVATION ON PAPER—STEP BY STEP

1. Place a paper towel, folded into three layers, on a plate. Spray the towel with water. Make sure that the paper lies flat.

2. Sprinkle seeds over the paper.

3. Mist the seeds so they're all completely damp.

4. Cover the seeds with plastic wrap. Don't make the cover airtight—or, make a few holes in the plastic.

5. Mist the seeds at least twice daily. Remove the plastic wrap and relocate the shoots to a spot with light once the shoots are growing.

6. Harvest, and enjoy!

light at this stage. However, they don't require total darkness to develop well.

Keep a close eye on the seeds from here on out; the drawback to paper is that it doesn't retain moisture as well as soil does, so make sure the paper and seeds don't dry out. Mist the seeds two to three times daily. The seeds should be damp but not swimming in water. How often they need to be misted also depends on indoor temperature and moisture levels in the air.

The seeds start splitting after a day or two. By all means, let the sprouts grow a tiny little bit ($\frac{1}{32}$–$\frac{2}{32}$ inches) before you place them in the light—preferably on a windowsill, but near a window will also work. A south-facing location with maximum light is ideal, but other directions will also do fine.

The plastic wrap can stay on for a day or two since it helps conserve moisture. Over the colder months, it also maintains the small amount of heat generated by the shoots under the wrap. But in summer, your priority is to make sure it doesn't get too hot for the seeds and that they don't dry out, so it's better to leave the plastic off.

Continue to mist the seeds two to three times daily to keep them damp.

Water

Seeds that just have to grow into shoots require only two things: light and water. That's why hydroponic cultivation, i.e., growing in water, is smart. Seeds are placed on a mesh grid that rests on a tray with water. The roots grow out and downward in search of the water, after which the seeds more or less take care of themselves. The only thing you must do is change the water and wash out the tray occasionally to keep it clean. If the shoots were to grow into plants, they would then need some type of nutrition, either from soil or, as in classic hydroponic cultivation, from nutrients delivered through the water. But there is no reason to add any extra nutrients to shoots that are only going to grow for, at most, three weeks. What's needed is already present in the seed itself, and light and water are the only two things we need to supply.

Personally, I think that that hydroponic cultivation is best suited to larger seeds, such as yellow and green peas and mung beans. They take a bit longer to grow, so it's a bonus that they look after themselves because the roots draw up all the water they need.

The industry sells special trays with grids. Those are made for larger seeds like beans and peas; there are also finer-meshed grids meant for small seeds.

With a bit of ingenuity, you can grow using a multiplaned sprouting tower by hydroponic cultivation. The tower can't be stacked, but each level can be used separately. Place one plane in a bigger rimmed container—a jelly roll or pie pan, for example. Add water so the plane is situated right above the water and the seeds can quickly let their roots find their way through the holes to the water below.

How to: Choose a container or mesh grid according to your seeds' size. Place the mesh grid over the water tray (or put a plane from a sprouting tower in a pan). Add water to reach just under the plane or the mesh grid. Spread seeds (dry or presoaked, depending on seed type) evenly and somewhat close together over the mesh grid. Mist the seeds with a flower mister so all seeds are moist.

Cover the seeds loosely with plastic wrap (or if airtight, make a few small holes in the plastic). Place the seed container by the sink—the spot doesn't need to be dark, but don't place the seeds in direct sunlight. Make sure the seeds are kept damp by misting them once or twice a day. After a few days—depending on the type of seeds—sprouts emerge. Wait one or two days to let the sprouts grow some more, then relocate them to the light on a windowsill or by a window. They will grow a little faster in a south-facing spot but, really, any window will do.

After a day or two, the shoots' roots will begin to find their way to the water. At this point, you can remove the mesh grid, wash out the basin, fill it up with clean water, and carefully replace the mesh grid. Try to gently put all the roots back inside the edge of the basin.

Make a habit of washing out and changing the water every day or every other day, and mist the seeds a few times over the first few days. The shoots will manage just fine on their own once the roots are in the water.

How to Harvest
Once the first leaves (the cotyledons) have developed, it's time to harvest the shoots. Just cut off what you need and let everything else continue to grow. Flavor and texture will change as the shoots grow; first, the delicate taste disappears, of course, but the shoots are typically good until the next set of leaves begin to emerge (and sometimes even longer). Harvest the shoots as needed, because they are tastiest and crispiest immediately after being cut. And isn't that just what the whole point is—harvesting and enjoying these shoots directly?

How to Store
Certain shoots, like arugula and broccoli, can grow for longer without their taste or texture suffering. Their flavor can even improve and become more distinctive with time. Other shoots, like mustard, chia, and radish, are most delicate when tender. If you don't have the opportunity to eat all the shoots when they're at their best, set the entire tray in the refrigerator to slow their growth significantly. That way you can harvest the shoots at your own pace over several days. This method works well with shoots that quickly go limp after harvesting.

Larger shoots, like sunflower and pea shoots, keep well long after harvesting. They will become stringy and coarse in texture if they're left to grow for too long. Instead, harvest them and store them in an aerated bag or box in the refrigerator. Are they looking sad? Rinse them or let them sit in cold water for a bit and they'll perk right up. The shoots can also be stored in a glass of water in the refrigerator.

The Swedish physician and cookbook author Charles Emil Hagdahl gave advice about cress cultivation as far back as in 1896 in his book *Kok-konsten som vetenskap och konst* (*Cuisine as Science and Art Form*):

"The seeds grow so easily that you can enjoy cress year-round, because during winter they are sown in boxes, on moss or on plates filled with soil, and they can have their assigned space in the kitchen. You can even moisten blotting paper or pieces of woolen cloth and sow seeds on them, and you will soon harvest cress if they're kept in a warm place. A bottle wrapped in damp flax or hemp scrap yarn, sown with cress seed, will soon be transformed into a flowering pyramid."

SHOOT PROFILES

ALFALFA

Most people think of sprouts when you mention alfalfa. But its seeds can also grow into perky shoots. Alfalfa seeds are cheap, easy to find, and very fast-growing—in other words, they're a smart way to enjoy green shoots year-round.

SUITABLE FOR

The shoots have a similar, slightly pealike flavor to the sprouts, while being a bit less earthy-tasting. They're good in salads, on sandwiches, or mixed in with smoothies. Or use them when making fruit and vegetable juices.

WHERE TO FIND THEM

Use the same seeds as for sprouting. The seeds are available at larger grocery stores, online, and in health food stores.

METHOD

Grow alfalfa directly on paper. The seeds don't need to soak; sow them directly on wet paper.

HOW TO

Use the paper method. The shoots are ready to be cut after four to six days. If you want to slow their growth, just place the container in the refrigerator and harvest them as needed.

Soaking time: No soaking required.
When to harvest: After 4 to 6 days
Seed amount needed: 1 tbsp of seeds is enough for one container measuring approximately 7" (18 cm) in diameter.

BROCCOLI

Broccoli shoots are fast and easy to grow and are hardy in both heat and cold. They belong to the cabbage family and so they do emit the smell of cabbage as they grow. However, the shoots' flavor is surprisingly mild.

Scientific research has shown broccoli shoots to be active protectors against certain forms of cancer. Broccoli contains sulforaphane, a compound it uses to protect itself; cannily enough, we use it this way, too. The more mature the broccoli, the less sulforaphane it has, so even if fully grown broccoli is very tasty, we'd get 20 to 50 times more of the healthy compound from its shoots.

SUITABLE FOR

Cabbage shoots have a mild taste and aren't as distinctly cabbage-y as fully grown broccoli or any other cabbage relative. Mix it in a smoothie with berries and fruit, snip it into salad, or sprinkle a cottage cheese sandwich with shoots and herb salt.

WHERE TO FIND THEM

Some health food stores will carry them, but they can be found primarily on health food websites. Just Google *broccoli sprouts*.

METHOD

The easiest way is to sow them directly onto paper. Broccoli seeds can also be grown as sprouts in a glass jar or in a colander, which is smart when you want to mix up a smoothie and wish to use the entire thing, seed and sprout.

HOW TO

Use the paper method. After only a day or two, small sprouts will emerge. Remove the plastic wrap, if using, and move the seeds to where they catch the light. The shoots will be ready after five to seven days. Harvest them as needed by cutting them as close to the paper as possible (or pull them up with seed, roots and all, and use the whole thing). The broccoli shoots remain delicate and delicious for several more days; however, some believe they're best when they grow their second pair of leaves, when the "true leaves" have just developed.

Soaking time: No soaking required.
When to harvest: After 5 to 7 days
Seed amount needed: 1 tbsp seeds is enough for a container measuring approx. 7" (18 cm) in diameter.

<< *Broccoli shoots ready to be harvested.*

YELLOW AND GREEN PEAS

Such winners! I never cease to be impressed by how these humble, small, dry peas can flourish into imposingly tall, winding shoots. They do take their time, naturally, but they are well worth the wait.

SUITABLE FOR

The rule of thumb is that a larger seed will turn out a larger shoot. Peas are large compared to arugula or alfalfa seeds, for example. They grow tall, mild shoots with a pealike sweetness. In restaurants, almost every other dish is garnished with pea shoots. It's easy to see why: a few slinky shoots can make any salad, soup, or meat entree look extra pretty.

WHERE TO FIND THEM

Regular dried yellow peas used for making soup can be found in any grocery store. Dried green peas are less common, but you'll be able to find them in a well-stocked store. Peas that are labeled "quick cooking" have been processed and will not grow. Also, don't try to grow peas that are split in half.

METHOD

Grow yellow and green peas in soil or hydroponically. While both methods work well, soil could have an advantage if you wish to harvest shoots a second time, since the seeds get their nutrients from the soil.

HOW TO

Use the soil or hydroponic method.

Regardless of the method you use, rinse and then soak the seeds in cold water for at least twelve hours beforehand. The soak doesn't just start the germination; it also helps you find and remove the peas that won't grow. After soaking, roll the peas about; the peas that are swollen are happily on their way. Pull out any of the peas that are still the same size as when you put them to soak. Toss any damaged or discolored peas, too.

Transfer the peas to a mesh grid if you are growing hydroponically, otherwise over the soil. Press lightly on the peas to make sure they are securely in the soil. Cover with plastic wrap, and preferably a kitchen towel, depending on which method you've chosen. Mist the peas occasionally with a flower mister, but make sure the soil is damp, not soaking wet.

After two to four days, you can see small sprouts emerge. Now's the time to move the container into the light.

Depending on the season and available light, the shoots will be ready for harvest between day 9 and 12. Cut the shoots right under the tiny leaves at the bottom of the stems.

However, if you want a second harvest, cut the shoots right above the second pair of leaves, further up the stem. This procedure can be repeated once more, but for each harvest the flavor will become lighter since the soil is being depleted. If the shoots are grown in water, you'll have to taste them to decide if they're worth harvesting several times.

Pea shoots are robust and hardy, not at all delicate like smaller shoots. They become stringy and dull if they grow too tall, so it's better to harvest them in a timely fashion and store the shoots in a box or a plastic bag in the refrigerator. The container should not be airtight—let the shoots breathe. They'll retain their freshness for up to two weeks in the refrigerator. If they look a bit droopy, give them a quick rinse or a bracing dip in a bowl of cold water.

Soaking time: 12 to 24 hours
When to harvest: 9 to 12 days
Seed amount needed: 1¾ fl oz (½ dl) is enough for a container measuring approx. 7" (18 cm) in diameter.

CRESS

There's something special about cress. Long before the term microgreens was on everyone's lips, cress seeds sprouted on a strip of cotton or a piece of paper towel. I, for one, am transported back to my childhood kitchen by cress's peppery scent. And it's a fun shoot to grow if you have kids around, because it's quick, easy, and has just that right amount of zing.

SUITABLE FOR

Cress is suitable anywhere you want a bit of peppery freshness. It's easy to get hooked and want a few snips now and then, like on a cheese sandwich at breakfast, or a potato pancake, or a slice of pie, or why not on a taco instead of cilantro? Try cress in herb butter along with flavor pals garlic or grated lemon peel.

WHERE TO FIND THEM

Seeds for garden cress, also known as poor man's pepper, pepperwort, and pepper grass, can be found at the grocery store, the plant nursery, in health food stores, and on Internet sites dedicated to cultivating. There are also other tasty cress varieties such as watercress and winter cress. However, seeds for those types of cress are sold in smaller amounts and are meant for longer cultivation than microgreens, which tends to make them more expensive.

METHOD

The paper method is obvious in this case. Soil and hydroponic methods work, too, but since the shoots grow so fast and taste best when they are tender, it's more convenient to grow them on paper. The seeds produce a gel coating so avoid soaking them; instead, spread them directly on wet paper.

HOW TO

Choose the paper method, as described above. Cress grows quickly and can be harvested as soon as after four to five days. The strong peppery flavor diminishes gradually, so it's purely up to you and your personal preference whether you wish to harvest the cress right away or wait; the flavor is milder around the tenth day.

When the flavor is at its best, you can put the tray in the refrigerator. The cress will still be fresh, but its growth will be almost completely halted. Cut shoots droop quickly, so cut them as needed.

Soaking time: No soaking required.
When to harvest: 4 to 5 days
Seed amount needed: 1 tbsp of seeds is enough for a container measuring approx. 7" (18 cm) in diameter.

ARUGULA

Although its name is Italian, arugula thrives in colder climates and is ideal for growing into shoots, especially during the winter months. Perhaps this is less surprising when you discover that arugula has been grown in Sweden for several centuries, albeit under the not-quite-as-charming moniker "mustard cabbage." It wasn't until the 1990s that arugula, under its Italian name, became one of the trendiest salad greens.

SUITABLE FOR

The shoots aren't as peppery as full-grown arugula; they have a mild, almost nutlike flavor. Snip it over a tomato salad or sprinkle it over an avocado sandwich. The shoots provide a nice touch of color and flavor to not only pesto but to other cold sauces and dips as well.

WHERE TO FIND THEM

Arugula seeds for microgreen cultivation can be purchased online; Google *rucola seed*. Packets with seeds meant for growing mature plants can be used for shoots, of course, but those packets contain so few seeds that it would be a pretty expensive way to do it.

METHOD

It's best to grow arugula on paper. You can also grow it in soil and hydroponically, which works well when you want the shoots to grow a little past the cotyledon stage.

HOW TO

Select your preferred method. Remember that arugula seeds produce a gel-like substance, so grow them directly on paper, some soil, or a mesh grid (for hydroponic cultivation) without them soaking first. The shoots are hardy at low temperatures but are sensitive to strong sunlight. Let the shoots be in light in the summer months, but avoid direct sunlight on hot days. If the shoots begin turning yellow, the light is too intense, so move them into partial shade.

At what stage the shoots are at their best is a matter of individual taste. Test the shoots when the first leaves appear, which takes about a week. If the leaves taste bitter, let the shoots grow a few more days. The nutty arugula taste will blossom as they grow.

Soaking time: No soaking required.
When to harvest: Approximately 7 days
Seed amount needed: 1 tbsp of seeds is enough for a container measuring approx. 7" (18 cm) in diameter.

RADISH (DAIKON)

A clear favorite that has a zippy, peppery bite and tiny shoots with real radish flavor. Even better, it's one of the fastest growing shoots and is ready to harvest after four to five days.

SUITABLE FOR

Sprinkle some snipped shoots over salads, stews, soups, pies—wherever you want a bit of color and life, really. The shoots taste distinctly of radish, but not with the peppery bite that some fully grown radishes can have. Mix them into salads, top your sandwiches with them, or add them to cold sauces and dips.

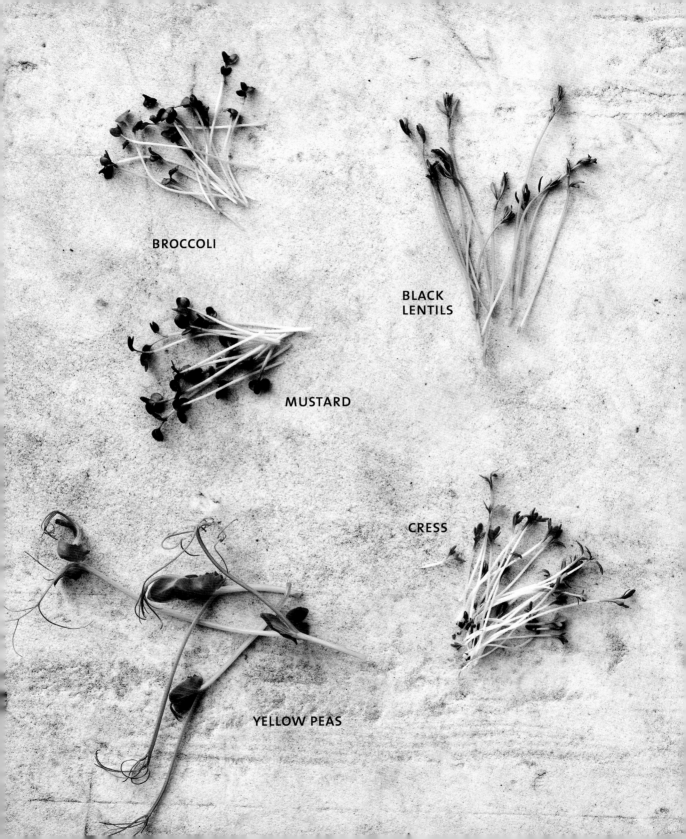

BROCCOLI

BLACK
LENTILS

MUSTARD

CRESS

YELLOW PEAS

CHIA

ALFALFA

ARUGULA

SUNFLOWER

RADISH

MUNG BEANS

WHERE TO FIND THEM

Online stores and plant nurseries are your primary sources for seeds intended for microgreen cultivation; however, you might also find them in health food stores. There are several types. Seeds are sold both as radish and daikon seeds, but they are just variations of the same plant (*raphanus sativus* is the Latin name). What they have in common is fast growth and a characteristic flavor. Their colors differ, however: China rose has pink stems and green leaves, sango is dark lilac, and daikon has completely green shoots.

METHOD

Growing on paper is the preferred method. It will work in soil and water, too, but since the shoots grow so quickly and taste better when they are tender, it's more practical to grow them on paper.

HOW TO

Choose the paper method. When the seeds begin to germinate, you'll notice some white fuzz around the emerging sprouts. This is perfectly normal, so don't confuse it with mold. The white fuzz are the shoots' very delicate roots starting to develop.

The radish shoots are at their best just when the first leaves appear. They will taste fine for a few days, but once the shoot starts to go for its true pair of leaves, the stalk's texture becomes a bit fibrous and threadlike. To be on the safe side, move the growing shoots to the refrigerator as soon as the cotyledon leaves have appeared. Of course, they will continue to grow in the refrigerator, but the process slows to a crawl so the shoots stay tender and delicate for up to two weeks.

Soaking time: No soaking required.
When to harvest: 4 to 6 days
Seed amount needed: 1 tbsp of seeds is enough for a container measuring approx. 7" (18 cm) in diameter.

MUSTARD SEEDS

Yellow and brown mustard seeds grow into fine shoots in about a week. Yellow seeds produce larger shoots, with leaves shifting to a dark red wine color underneath. The shoots have a somewhat mild yet clear, pronounced flavor. Brown seeds produce shoots with intense and classic mustard character. Most of the zip is in the stems so, if you want a milder taste, just use the leaves. It's worth mentioning, however, that the strong flavor indicates that the stems contain fine protective compounds that are good for us. Yellow shoots grow slightly faster than brown shoots, but only beat them by a day or two.

SUITABLE FOR

Mustard shoots work best as a spice and seasoning. Wherever you typically use mustard, add shoots as a fun replacement. Snip them over a ham sandwich or sprinkle them over sausage or pea soup. Julienned shoots also add good zip to sauces and dressings.

WHERE TO FIND THEM

Brown and yellow mustard seeds can be found on the spice shelf of the grocery store. The brown seeds are smaller than the yellow seeds.

METHOD

The simplest way to grow them is on paper, but soil cultivation works also.

HOW TO

Select your method. Mustard seeds require no presoaking. The yellow seeds are larger and grow a bit faster. Don't mistake the white fuzz that develops around the seed for mold—they're the shoots' delicate, threadlike roots.

Yellow mustard seeds are ready to harvest after four to five days; the brown seeds usually take an extra day or two.

Soaking time: No soaking required.
When to harvest: 5 to 7 days
Seed amount needed: 1 tbsp of seeds is enough for a container measuring approx. 7" (18 cm) in diameter.

SUNFLOWER SEEDS

Sunflower shoots are perfect if you want to grow your own salad. The shoots are sturdy with juicy, slightly nutty-flavored leaves. But it's a little bit tricky to grow them successfully. They require a lot of care if all seeds are to start and grow upward. And the temperature needs to be a bit warmer—the shoots will go on strike if they're too cold.

SUITABLE FOR

The shoots have a nutlike flavor and hardly any bitterness, so they are suitable for all kinds of salads. Add some to your sandwich, sprinkle them over soup, or mix them into a green smoothie.

WHERE TO FIND THEM

To grow shoots, buy seeds in their hull. The best seeds have black hulls; these are primarily sold online.

Zippy, peppery radish shoots. >>

SUNFLOWER SHOOTS, STEP-BY-STEP

1. Rinse off the sunflower seeds, and then soak them for 24 hours.

2. Drain the soaked seeds in a sieve.

3. Place the sieve over a bowl. Cover the bowl with plastic wrap, but loosely—not airtight.

4. Let the seeds grow for about 48 hours. Rinse two to three times every 24 hours.

5. Cut a milk carton in half lengthwise and fill it with potting soil.

6. Spread the sprouts evenly over the soil.

7. Press slightly with your hand to anchor the sprouts to the soil.

8. Mist lightly with water.

9. Cover with the second half of the milk carton, and place a light weight on top.

10. Let the sprouts grow, covered, for about 48 hours at 69.8°F to 77°F (21°C–25°C). Remove the upper part of the milk carton. Mist lightly.

11. Place the shoots in the light. Keep the soil damp and consistently warm. Water now and then.

12. Taste after a while to determine when it's time to harvest.

Seeds with gray-and-white-striped hulls are usable, but they're at a disadvantage compared to the black ones. The stripy hulls may be bigger and so will produce bigger shoots, but their shells are so hard and cling so tenaciously to the seed that it can be difficult to remove them. Seeds sold as bird seed can also be used, but they are not presorted so there's usually a lot of dirt in the mix. Also, quite a few of the seeds tend to be damaged. Those need to be removed or they might rot while the other seeds are growing.

Hulled seeds can also be used for cultivation. Their advantage is that you don't have to pick out the hulls at harvest. However, you'd be taking a big risk because germination rates vary widely. The hulled seeds need to be kept cold for preservation, but of course that's not done in grocery stores where they are not sold for the purpose of cultivation.

METHOD
Grow in soil. Hydroponic works, but it's chancier. Follow the process below as it's a little bit tricky to grow sunflower shoots successfully.

HOW TO
Follow the soil method. Rinse the seeds under the tap with cold water. Remove any dirt and damaged seeds. Soak the seeds in cold water for 24 hours. Some will float to the surface; place a weight on the surface so all seeds remain submerged. The easiest way to do this is to fill plastic bags with a cup or two of water and set them on top to press the seeds down. Soaking softens the shell and starts the germination process.

Place the seeds in a sieve and rinse them under the tap with cold water. Turn the seeds carefully and remove any remaining dirt or damaged seeds. Place the sieve over a bowl and cover loosely—not airtight—with plastic wrap. Rinse the seeds two or three times every 24 hours, and make sure the seeds stay damp at all times. After 24 to 48 hours most of the seeds will have cracked and small sprouts emerged. The seeds are now ready to cultivate. If there are no visible sprouts, wait another 24 hours. Don't let the sprouts grow too long, because they are very delicate and will easily break off.

Choose a container that can be filled with potting soil. Bottom drainage is not necessary; it usually works fine if you're just careful not to overwater. Fill your container—a milk carton cut in half lengthwise, for example—with a generous 1-inch (3 cm) layer of soil. Mist the soil lightly with water. Spread the sprouts over the soil and pat them down gently with your hand so they're anchored in the soil. Mist with water again. Cover the sprouts with the other half of the milk carton (upside-down, so it's pressed down on the sprouts). Place a small weight, like a glass or a can, on top. This helps the sprouts orient themselves properly, i.e., down into the soil. The sprouts thrive in a temperature between 69.8°F and 77°F (21–25°C). They don't grow well if it's colder.

After about two days, the roots will have grown into the soil and the stalks begin to strain upward. Remove the top part of the milk carton and the weight. Place the shoots in the light in or near a window. Make sure the temperature stays between 69.8°F and 77°F (21–25°C). Mist the shoots carefully—they don't like too much moisture.

If you dare attempt to grow sunflower shoots during winter, the stalks will probably be taller and the leaves a bit thinner. The stalks stretch as far as they can to take in as much light as possible. In better lit conditions, the shoots will be shorter with thicker, juicier leaves. The light also provides the seed with the power to emerge and to shake off the shell that contains the pair of leaves. If the shell is too snug, try to help loosen it a bit.

Depending on the season and available light, it can take anywhere from six to twelve days from the time the seeds are placed on the soil till the shoots are ready to be harvested. The shoots are good from the moment the cotyledons appear until the next set of leaves start to show. You'll notice them creeping out at the top between the cotyledons. The shoots now go from tender, delicate, and juicy to more fibrous-y in texture and coarser in flavor.

It's better to cut off the shoots when they are at their peak and keep them in a plastic bag or box in the refrigerator. Don't close the container completely; make sure the shoots can breathe. After the shoots have been harvested, a second, smaller crop will grow. This one can be harvested after a few days.

Soaking time: 24 hours
When to harvest: 8 to 14 days (2 days are for sprouting in a sieve)
Seed amount needed: 2 tbsp seeds will be enough for a container measuring

approx. 8" x 2¾" (20 x 7 cm)—half a milk carton, for instance.

HERE ARE A FEW EXTRA SHOOTS THAT ARE WELL WORTH GROWING

CHIA SEEDS

This small South American seed has recently become a real trendy tidbit. And it's healthy, of course—just like every other seed, we might add. However, there's no consensus on how much of its wholesomeness we are actually able to absorb. Most of the seeds pass pretty much undigested through our system when we eat, say, chia pudding. But cultivating chia seeds into shoots is a good idea. The small seeds will produce a gel-like substance, so grow them directly on paper. Their progress is slower than that of other small seeds, so the shoots are not ready until after eight to ten days. Their flavor is neutral and mild. Snip them over a salad or soup, or mix them into a smoothie.

LENTILS

You can grow all types of lentils into shoots, as long as they haven't been pretreated in any way. The most practical way to do it is to spread the soaked lentils onto wet paper, but they will grow well in soil or water, too. The shoots have a mild, neutral flavor and are suitable for mixing in salads or into smoothies.

CORN KERNELS

Regular dried corn kernels grow into intensely sweet shoots. Cultivation is a bit hit-or-miss since not every kernel will germinate. But it's fun to try, and the sweet flavor is surprising and impressive. The shoots become attractively pinkish-green. Simply use regular dried corn kernels—those used for making popcorn. Avoid microwaveable corn or any other treated corn kernels. Soak the kernels for twelve hours. Grow in soil. Harvest the shoots when they're a generous 1 inch (3 cm) tall. A few days later, they'll turn into longish, slim leaves that are far too stringy in texture to eat—it would be like chewing grass.

Use the small, sweet shoots to sweeten a dish, like snipped over a fruit salad.

MUNG BEANS

The number-one sprouting bean can of course be grown into shoots. Just as with sprouting, it's important to soak the beans first. Grow the sprouts in soil or hydroponically. Spruce up your salad with these shoots that truly have a look all their own (see picture on p. 11).

RECIPES
SHOOTS &
MICROGREENS

SPICY APPLE KICK

Really tender shoots are best for smoothies. The shoots might get a bit fibrous if they're allowed to grow longer, at which point they're nicer for a salad.

MAKES 2 GLASSES

1 avocado

Approx. 6¾ fl oz (2 dl) pea shoots, or other mild shoots, for example from broccoli, sunflower, or chia seeds

1 tbsp grated fresh ginger

2 tbsp fresh mint leaves

1¼ cups apple juice, well chilled

1 tbsp freshly squeezed lemon juice

Halve the avocado, remove the stone, and scoop out the flesh. Mix all the ingredients to make a soft smoothie. Use a countertop blender if you have one, although an immersion blender will also work.

Pour into glasses.

STRAWBERRY SMOOTHIE WITH SHOOTS

This smoothie is velvety and satisfying, reminiscent of a shake. If the strawberries aren't sweet enough, it's a good idea to add a banana.

MAKES 2 GLASSES

Approx. 6¾ fl oz (2 dl) broccoli shoots, or other mild shoots from sunflower, pea, or chia seeds

6¾ fl oz (2 dl) frozen strawberries

1¼ cups (3 dl) almond milk (or oat milk)

2 tbsp peanut butter

1 banana (optional)

Using a countertop blender or an immersion blender, mix all the ingredients to make a velvety smoothie.

Pour into glasses.

BLACKBERRY SMOOTHIE WITH BROCCOLI & LIME

The blackberries' lilac color is evidence of their high content of wholesome antioxidants. Together with the healthiness of the broccoli shoots, this becomes a veritable super smoothie. If you have blueberries or black currants in the freezer, they will work just as well.

MAKES 2 GLASSES

Approx. 6¾ fl oz (2 dl) broccoli shoots, or other mild shoots such as sunflower, pea, or chia
6¾ fl oz (2 dl) frozen blackberries
6¾ fl oz (2 dl) plain mild yogurt (3%)
1 banana, frozen
½ tbsp freshly squeezed lime juice
⅕ tsp vanilla powder
1 tbsp liquid honey, if desired

Using a countertop blender (although an immersion blender will work too), blend all the ingredients to make a velvety smoothie.

Pour into glasses.

See picture on p. 106.

GREEN SMOOTHIE BOWL

Here's a bowl containing both sprouts and shoots. The buckwheat provides a little extra satiety. Top the bowl with some poppy seeds, grated coconut, nuts, and berries.

MAKES 2 BOWLS

Approx. 1¼ cup (3 dl) mild, tender shoots such as broccoli, chia, pea, or sunflower
2 frozen bananas
3½ oz (100 g) frozen mango, diced
2 tbsp buckwheat sprouts
6¾ fl oz (2 dl) mild plain yogurt (3%) or coconut or almond milk
Hemp hearts, poppy seeds, grated coconut, nuts, and frozen red and/or black currants, for topping

Blend shoots, bananas, mango, sprouted buckwheat, and yogurt until smooth using a countertop or immersion blender.

Pour into bowls and top with hemp hearts, poppy seeds, nuts, coconut, and berries.

FRESH SPRING ROLLS WITH RED CABBAGE, NUTS, AND MANGO

Super delicious rice paper rolls! They're a bit fussy to make, but once everything is in place, it goes smoothly. The red cabbage, mango, and shoots display beautiful colors when glimpsed through the paper.

SERVES 4 (MAKES 16 ROLLS)
3⅓ fl oz (1 dl) salted peanuts
1 tbsp sesame oil
1¾ fl oz (½ dl) canola oil
2 tbsp Japanese soy sauce
½ tsp sambal oelek
1 (7 oz [200 g]) wedge of red cabbage
2 avocados
1 tbsp freshly squeezed lime juice
3 red onions
2 mangoes
8 large rice papers
1 bunch of fresh mint leaves
Approx. 2¼ cups (5 dl) mixed shoots, such as pea, sunflower, and radish

Tip!

These rolls can be prepared a few hours in advance. Just cover them with the damp towel you used for rolling them. Store them in the refrigerator.

Coarsely chop the nuts in a food processor. Add in the sesame oil, canola oil, soy sauce, and sambal oelek. Simply give it a quick pulse so everything is mixed. Transfer to a bowl.

Julienne the red cabbage finely. Transfer to another bowl.

Halve the avocados, remove the stones, and slice the avocado flesh. Transfer to another bowl and add the lime juice to prevent the avocado from turning brown. Julienne the onions and transfer to a bowl. Peel and cut the mangoes into rectangular chunks.

Fill a large bowl or wide saucepan with lukewarm water. Wet a clean kitchen towel, wring it out, and place it on the kitchen counter. Dip one sheet of rice paper at a time in the water for about 30 seconds. Place the rice paper on the towel.

Put some red cabbage, avocado, onion, mango, shoots, and a few mint leaves in the middle of the sheet of rice paper. Drizzle with some sauce.

Start by folding the paper away from you, up and over the filling. Press down a little, carefully, and then fold in the sides. Roll.

Place the roll on a cutting board covered in a clean, dampened kitchen towel. Prepare the rest of the rolls in the same way. Set the rolls about ¼-inch apart so they don't stick to each other.

Cut each roll into two halves and transfer on a platter. Serve the rolls with Japanese soy sauce or a soy dip with mustard and sesame oil (see p. 73).

BROCCOLI WITH BLUE CHEESE AND HONEY-ROASTED PECANS

Raw broccoli might sound a bit chewy, but kneading olive oil and salt into it works wonders! The broccoli softens while remaining fresh and crisp.

SERVES 4

1¾ fl oz (½ dl) pecans
1 tbsp honey
2 stalks broccoli with florets
½ red onion
1 tsp salt
3 tbsp olive oil
1 apple
½ tbsp freshly squeezed lemon juice
6¾ fl oz (2 dl) broccoli shoots
3½ oz (100 g) blue cheese
Freshly ground black pepper

Roast the pecans in a dry, hot skillet for about 2 minutes. Add the honey and let it bubble while stirring for another 2 minutes, or until the honey is a golden color. Immediately pour the nuts onto a sheet of parchment paper, and separate the nuts so they don't clump together. Let cool.

Separate the broccoli into smaller florets, and slice the stalk into thin slices. Peel, halve, and slice the onion thinly.

Put the broccoli and onion in a bowl. Sprinkle with salt and oil. Knead and massage the broccoli with your hands for a few minutes, or until the broccoli has softened a little. You can also put it all in a plastic bag and knead from the outside.

Slice the apple thinly.

Transfer the broccoli mix and the apple slices onto a platter. Drizzle with lemon juice, and sprinkle with broccoli shoots and crumbled blue cheese. Top everything with the honey-roasted pecans and a few grinds of fresh black pepper.

ROASTED POTATO SALAD WITH MUSTARD SHOOTS

This salad is a proven winner! That's not surprising, since it has everything: it's tangy, salty, and creamy. The original recipe featured bacon, but I'm using sun-dried tomatoes here instead.

SERVES 4

2¼ lb (1 kg) small potatoes, preferably young potatoes
2 tbsp olive oil
Salt
1¾ fl oz (½ dl) sun-dried tomatoes
Olive oil, for frying
3 tbsp cider vinegar
½ tsp chopped fresh rosemary
3⅓ fl oz (1 dl) mayonnaise
1¾ fl oz (½ dl) chopped parsley
10 radishes
½ red onion
6¾ fl oz (2 dl) mustard shoots

Preheat the oven to 435°F (225°C).

Put the potatoes in a rimmed baking pan; if some potatoes are bigger than others, cut them in half. Drizzle with olive oil and season with salt. Bake on the middle rack of the oven for about 20 minutes, or until the potatoes are soft. Let cool.

Julienne the sun-dried tomatoes. In a skillet, sauté them quickly in some oil. Add half the vinegar, and cook for 2 minutes.

Mix the remaining vinegar with the rosemary, mayonnaise, and parsley.

Cut the radishes into thin slices. Peel and finely julienne the red onion.

Mix the potatoes with fried sun-dried tomatoes, mayonnaise mix, radishes, mustard shoots, and red onion.

SPIRALIZED SALAD WITH SHOOTS, GOAT CHEESE, AND ALMONDS

Spiralize more! For some reason, it's more fun to eat vegetables when they're cut into long strips than when they are grated. Beets and carrots are excellent flavor companions to mixed shoots.

SERVES 4

1¾ fl oz (½ dl) slivered almonds

14 oz (400 g) mixed beets—red, Chioggia, or golden beets, for example

2 carrots

2 tbsp olive oil

1 tsp salt flakes

⅕ tsp black pepper

1¼ cup (5 dl) mixed shoots such as arugula, mustard, and radish

5¼ oz (150 g) goat cheese

DRESSING

1 tbsp lemon juice, freshly squeezed

½ tbsp liquid honey

1 tbsp olive oil

⅕ tsp salt

Roast the almonds in a dry skillet until they are slightly golden. Let cool.

Peel and spiralize the beets and carrots with a spiralizer (or slice them on a mandoline, which makes the slices thin and delicious). Use scissors to shorten the strands here and there to make the salad easier to serve.

Mix the spiralized vegetables with oil, salt flakes, and pepper.

Layer the spiralized vegetables with shoots on a platter or in a bowl. Sprinkle with crumbled goat cheese and slivered almonds.

Mix the lemon juice with the honey, oil, and salt to make the dressing, and drizzle it over the salad.

INDIAN KORMA WITH CAULIFLOWER AND PEA SHOOTS

The secret here is spelled B-U-T-T-E-R. Lots of it. And quite a lot of cream, too . . . This is a mild and satisfying stew featuring cauliflower and sprouted soybeans. Top it with crisp pea shoots.

SERVES 4

3½ oz (100 g) soybean sprouts
1 yellow onion
1 cauliflower, appr. 1¾ lb (800 g)
1 tsp whole cardamom
2¾ oz (75 g) butter
1 tbsp cumin
1¾ fl oz (½ dl) raisins (golden raisins would be great here)
1 tbsp turmeric
1 tbsp table sugar
1½ tsp salt
5 fl oz (1½ dl) water
5 fl oz (1½ dl) heavy whipping cream
1 cup (2½ dl) almond flour
3⅓ fl oz (1 dl) grated coconut
1¼ cups (3 dl) plain yogurt (3%)
Ground black pepper
Salt, to taste
6¾ fl oz (2 dl) pea shoots

Cook the soybeans in lightly salted water for 15 minutes. Let them drain.

Peel and finely chop the onion. Cut up the cauliflower. Save the leaves; julienne them finely and set them aside. Break the cauliflower into small florets.

Crush the cardamom finely with a mortar and pestle.

Melt the butter in a large skillet. On medium-high heat, fry the onion, cardamom, and cumin for 2 to 4 minutes while stirring.

Add the cauliflower, raisins, turmeric, sugar, and salt. Keep cooking and stirring for about 5 minutes.

Add the water, cream, almond flour, coconut, soybeans, and the cauliflower leaves. Cook for about 2 minutes.

Stir in the yogurt, and let everything simmer for 1 or 2 minutes. Season with pepper, and some more salt if needed. Top with pea shoots. This stew is great to serve with some naan bread, pickled lime or mango chutney, Turkish yogurt, and basmati rice.

CAESAR SALAD WITH KALE AND SHOOTS

Mix all different types of shoots to make a tangy Caesar salad. And add some kale, too, because it's so tasty. This will need some dressing, preferably a very creamy one.

SERVES 4–6

DRESSING

1 large egg yolk

1 crushed garlic clove

1 tbsp + ½ tsp lemon juice, freshly squeezed

1 tsp Dijon mustard

3⅓ fl oz (1 dl) canola oil

3⅓ fl oz (1 dl) olive oil

6¾ fl oz (2 dl) finely grated Pecorino cheese

Salt

Freshly ground black pepper

SALAD

10½ oz (300 g) kale

1¼ cups (5 dl) mixed shoots, such as sunflower, pea, and arugula

1¾ fl oz (½ dl) roasted sunflower seeds (or sunflower bark, see p. 83)

2 tbsp dried red/black currants (or blueberries)

Shaved Pecorino cheese, for serving

Start by making the dressing. Mix the egg yolk, garlic, 1 tablespoon of the lemon juice, and mustard with an immersion blender or in a food processor.

Add the canola oil, followed by the olive oil, in a thin stream while mixing continuously. Add the Pecorino cheese and season with salt and pepper.

Shred the kale into smaller pieces. Put the kale and the shoots in a bowl. Mix them with half of the dressing. Transfer to a platter.

Top with sunflower seeds, red/black currants, shaved Pecorino cheese, and dab on the remaining dressing.

AVOCADO MAYO WITH SHOOTS

A creamy dressing that goes with just about everything!

MAKES ABOUT 6¾ FL OZ (2 DL)
1 avocado
Approx. 6¾ fl oz (2 dl) mild shoots, such as rucola or broccoli
1 crushed garlic clove
Grated zest of ½ a lemon
1 tbsp of freshly squeezed lemon juice
1 tsp white wine vinegar
3½ fl oz (1 dl) mild olive oil
⅖ tsp salt
⅕ tsp freshly ground black pepper

Halve the avocado, remove the stone, and scoop out the flesh.

In a food processor or with an immersion blender, mix the avocado, shoots, garlic, lemon zest and juice, vinegar, oil, salt, and black pepper until smooth.

Tip!

If the dressing curdles, save it by adding in another egg yolk. Whisk the yolk lightly in a bowl. Add the curdled dressing, drop by drop, to the egg yolk while whisking.

APPLE SALSA AND MUSTARD SHOOTS FROM THE SKÅNE REGION

Here we've doubled up on the flavors with both brown mustard and mustard shoots. It's very tasty with a summer barbecue or at a buffet.

SERVES 4
2 tbsp olive oil
½ tbsp cider vinegar
½ tbsp brown mustard*
⅕ tsp salt
⅕ tsp freshly ground black pepper
1 red apple
10 cherry tomatoes
½ red onion
3⅓ fl oz (1 dl) mustard shoots
*If you have access to Skåne mustard, I highly recommend you use it here!

Mix the oil, vinegar, mustard, salt, and pepper together to make the dressing.

Cut the apple into small dice. Cut the tomatoes into smaller chunks. Peel and slice the onion thinly.

Mix the apple, tomatoes, and red onion with the dressing. Let the mix stand for at least 20 minutes.

Fold in the mustard shoots before serving.

HERBY CRESS BUTTER

I like butter. And cress. They are sooo delicious when paired together. Enjoy this compound butter with bread, with something grilled, or dab it onto roasted root vegetables.

SERVES 4
3½ oz (100 g) butter
6¾ fl oz (2 dl) cress
Grated zest from 1 lemon
½ tsp salt flakes

Let the butter stand at room temperature to soften a little. Put the butter in a bowl and whisk it with an electric handheld beater until light and airy.

Mince the cress very finely.

Mix the lemon zest, cress, and salt with the butter. To keep the butter together, transfer it to a sheet of parchment paper and roll into a tube. Store it in the refrigerator or freezer.

See picture on previous page.

ROASTED ALMOND PESTO WITH ARUGULA SHOOTS & LEMON

Arugula shoots and roasted almonds make a superb pesto! Add some grated lemon zest to liven it up.

MAKES ABOUT 6¾ FL OZ (2 DL)
3⅓ fl oz (1 dl) almonds
Approx. 6¾ fl oz (2 dl) arugula shoots
1–2 garlic cloves, crushed
3⅓ fl oz (1 dl) grated Parmesan cheese
3⅓ fl oz (1 dl) olive oil
Grated zest of ½ lemon
½ tsp salt
⅕ tsp freshly ground black pepper

Roast the almonds in a dry skillet for about 3 minutes, or until they are nicely colored. Stir them from time to time so they don't burn. Let cool.

Mix the almonds, arugula shoots, and crushed garlic in short bursts in a food processor or with an immersion blender. Add the Parmesan and oil, and continue to mix until it makes a thick pesto.

Stir in the grated lemon zest, salt, and pepper.

See picture on previous page.

INDEX

RECIPE INDEX

ACKNOWLEDGMENTS

My most heartfelt thank you goes out to two highly accomplished nutritionists for all the knowledge you shared with me—Karin Jonsson at Chalmers, and Monika Pearson, formerly of the Swedish National Food Administration. And also to Baljväxtakademin—the Swedish Legume Academy—for your enthusiastic participation!

To my wonderful colleagues at *Buffé*, for letting me bounce ideas around with you. And extra thanks goes to you, Sofia Nilsson, for your assistance with the recipes and staging. You're the world's smartest, speediest, and coolest chef!

Photographer Lennart "Lelle" Weibull, because you saw the living beauty in burgeoning shoots—and managed to capture it in photographs. And graphic designer Pernilla Qvist, who took pictures and text and made them flow beautifully. And to you, Swedish editor Anna Sodini and Swedish book publisher Eva Kruk, for your guidance, your pep, and most of all, for your belief in my idea for this book.

The ceramics artist Calle Forsberg, who let me use his gorgeous bowls and plates—it's as if they were made for sprouts and shoots! Thanks also to the companies Himla, Room, and Blås & Knåda for lending us such exquisite things.

And finally, to Henrik, Malva, Ellen, and Olle, a brave family that has eaten its way through all the dishes—many times—and that was occasionally crowded out of the kitchen due to growing shoots in different stages, everywhere.

SOURCES

Studies on protein quality in legumes with special reference to factors interfering with protein utilization and digestibility of brown beans (Phaseolus vulgaris L). Monika Lövgren, Uppsala Universitetet 1988

Nutritional changes in seeds during germination—with focus on product development. Karin Jonsson. Chalmers University of Technology.

Nutrition, sensory, quality and safety evaluation of a new speciality produce: Microgreens. Zhenlei Xiao, University of Maryland, 2013

History of sprouts. William Shurtleff and Akiko Aoyagi, Soyinfo Center, Lafayette, California, USA, 2013

Råd om mat för barn 0-5 år - vetenskaptligt underlag med risk - eller nyttovärderingar och kunskapsöversikter. Rapport 21/2011 från Statens Livsmedelsverk.*

Råd om mat för barn 0-5 år - hanteringsrapport som beskriver hur risk-och nyttovärderingar, tillsammans med andra faktorer, har lett fram till Livsmedelsverkets råd. Rapport 22/2011 från Statens Livsmedelsverk.*

[* Only published in Swedish]

CONVERSION CHARTS

METRIC AND IMPERIAL CONVERSIONS
(These conversions are rounded for convenience)

Ingredient	Cups/Tablespoons/Teaspoons	Ounces	Grams/Milliliters
Butter	1 cup = 16 tablespoons = 2 sticks	8 ounces	230 grams
Cheese, shredded	1 cup	4 ounces	110 grams
Cream cheese	1 tablespoon	0.5 ounce	14.5 grams
Cornstarch	1 tablespoon	0.3 ounce	8 grams
Flour, all-purpose	1 cup/1 tablespoon	4.5 ounces/0.3 ounce	125 grams/8 grams
Flour, whole wheat	1 cup	4 ounces	120 grams
Fruit, dried	1 cup	4 ounces	120 grams
Fruits or veggies, chopped	1 cup	5 to 7 ounces	145 to 200 grams
Fruits or veggies, pureed	1 cup	8.5 ounces	245 grams
Honey, maple syrup, or corn syrup	1 tablespoon	0.75 ounce	20 grams
Liquids: cream, milk, water, or juice	1 cup	8 fluid ounces	240 milliliters
Oats	1 cup	5.5 ounces	150 grams
Salt	1 teaspoon	0.2 ounce	6 grams
Spices: cinnamon, cloves, ginger, or nutmeg (ground)	1 teaspoon	0.2 ounce	5 milliliters
Sugar, brown, firmly packed	1 cup	7 ounces	200 grams
Sugar, white	1 cup/1 tablespoon	7 ounces/0.5 ounce	200 grams/12.5 grams
Vanilla extract	1 teaspoon	0.2 ounce	4 grams

OVEN TEMPERATURES

Fahrenheit	Celsius	Gas Mark
225°	110°	¼
250°	120°	½
275°	140°	1
300°	150°	2
325°	160°	3
350°	180°	4
375°	190°	5
400°	200°	6
425°	220°	7
450°	230°	8